THROUGH

THE

NARROW GATE

The surprising door into radiant life

THE SKY FAMILY

ISBN 978-1479231737

table of contents

LESSON 1 1

Why Am I So Empty? The Blessing, The Curse,
Why Is Law So Important?

LESSON 2 5

The Blessing And Penalty Of The Law, Without A Penalty
There Is No Law, Obeying The Law Brings Blessing,
The Penalty Is Strict, But Delayed, God's Laws Are Radioactive!
God's Laws Govern The Heart, Learning About The Penalty,
Enter Jesus, Jesus Stops The Cycle Of Sin And Death.

LESSON 3 12

So What Are God's Laws? The 10 Commandments,
The First and Second Commandments Alone Explain
Our Condition, False Gods, And What Is The Punishment?
It Is God Trying To Save Our Lives,
Our False Gods Will Lead Us To A True Hell.

LESSON 4 18

Christianity, The Religion Of Grace, Religion Of Works,
Christianity Is Not Based On How Well We Keep The Laws Of God,
Sin Separates Us From God, The Quicksand Effect,
Jesus himself Reaches Out To Us.

LESSON 5 23

Jesus' Salvation, How Do I Get Saved? Admit In Your Heart
That You Are A Sinner, Admit Your Need For A Savior,
Confess Your Sins, Ask Him To Save You, Believe In Your Heart,
Confess With Your Mouth, Receive It By Faith, Be Baptized,
Be Putting To Death The Deeds Of Sin, Just Talk To God,
How To Pray, Faith.

LESSON 6 30

The Transition Of The Law, Two Meanings Of Law,
The Ceremonial Law Was Replaced By The Coming Of Jesus,
There Is Also A Change In The Other Law, The 10 Commandments
Stand Apart, The Law Is God's Standard Of Righteousness,
The Commandments Become The Rule Of Life.

LESSON 7 37

The Devil's Job, Our Human Nature Works With Him,
Obedience Is Better Than Repentance,
Disobedience Always Brings Punishment.

LESSON 8 41

The Third Commandment, Do Not Follow The Multitude In Doing Evil,
God Does Not Forget Because It Is His Name, Picture This,
Other Uses Of Swearing Prohibited By The Commandment,
Fascinating Fact.

LESSON 9 47

The Class Room, Mediums And Spiritists, More Interesting Laws,
Ill Gotten Gains Do Not Profit.

LESSON 10 53

The Fourth Commandment, The Rules Of The House,
The Heart Of This Law, It Is A Commandment Of Major Importance To God,
The Corruption Of The Commandment, The Dreaded Sabbath,
The Day For Worldly Indulgence, Family Time, The True Father,
True Worship On The Lord's Day.

LESSON 11 61

Call The Sabbath A Delight, Going To Church, Your Own Pleasure,
Speaking Idle Words, Take Delight In The Lord,
Entering The Presence Of God, It Takes Time And Energy,
God Cannot Be Had By The Easily Distracted, Your Adversary,
The World Won't Make Time For You To Be With God, Long Distance,
Why Do We Celebrate The Sabbath On Sunday?
Did Paul Speak Against The Sabbath?

LESSON 12 70

The Fifth Commandment, Frightening Scriptures,
The Great Net, Parents Take The Place Of God.

LESSON 13 75

The Sixth Commandment, Thou Shalt Not Murder, Killing VS. Murdering,
Two Degrees Of Murder, The Heart Attitude Determines The Crime, It's So
Easy To Break This Law, The Rambo Effect, Love Thy Enemies, Murder In
Sports, The Spirit Of Murder Prevails, Blessed Are The Peacemakers.

LESSON 14 83

The Seventh Commandment, Thou Shalt Not Commit Adultery,
Do Not Follow The Multitude In Doing Evil, Her House Is The Way To Hell,
God Removes His Spirit, Why Is It So Wrong?,
Lust is The Opposite Of Love, God's Blessing On Fidelity.

LESSON 15 89

The Atoms Of Society, Jesus' Definition, Unfaithful Thoughts,
Women's Magazines, To Adulterate, Working For The Devil,
Modesty, The Forgotten Virtue, No Excuse, Modesty In Speech.

LESSON 16 95

Camp Of The Canaanites, How Do I Get Out? More Scriptural Warnings,
Help For Those Already Destroyed By Adultery.

LESSON 17 101

The Eighth Commandment: Thou Shalt Not Steal,
Beware Of Greed In All Its Forms, Returning Lost Items: An Amazing Story,
Taxes, Think About This, Your Time At Work, Three Examples,
More Things To Be Careful Of, Will You Rob God?
The Supernatural Dimension, The Joy Of Obeying,
The Heart Of the Commandment.

LESSON 18 112

The Ninth Commandment, Thou Shalt Not Bear False
Witness Against Thy Neighbor, The Cheiftan,
Lies Destroy The Joy Of Society, Half Truths, Backbiting,
The Searchlight, The Accuser Of The Brethren,
Obeying The Heart Of This Commandment,
Love Thy Enemy, Are You Kidding?

LESSON 19 120

The Tenth Commandment: Thou Shalt Not Covet,
God's Word To The Church, Cattle, What Cattle?,
This Speaks To The Church Today, What The Bible Has To Say,
A Single Eye, False Prophets, False Prophets Don't Know It,
His Children's Lifestyle, Thy Neighbor's Wife,
Anything That Belongs To Your Neighbor, Jesus Walked.

LESSON 20 129

Our Freedom In Christ, Our Freedom To Be Good,
Our Freedom Is The Cross, A King's Ransom, Our Selfless King,
Our Own Agenda, Love And Selfishness Cancel Each Other,
Loving God, Loving Our Neighbor, Bear The Insult,
The Secret Power Of God, Stand Up For Yourself?

LESSON 21 141

Taking Up Our Cross Daily, How Much Is Your Soul Worth?
The Servant Of All, The Cross Is The Attraction, The Passions Of The Flesh,
Lawful Pleasures, Exceeding The Speed Limit, What Is The Speed Limit?
Everything In Moderation, Our Pleasure Is Where Our Heart Is,
Nothing But Christ.

LESSON 22 151

Laying Aside Every Encumbrance, Distractions, The Beggar Prince,
Your Thoughts Determine Your Relationship, The Test,
The Seed, The Fellowship Of The Unashamed, The Commitment,
It Shall Not Fasten it's Grip On Me.

LESSON 23 160

Ssshhh, Sleeping Virgins! Various End Time Scenarios,
The Gospels Take Precedence, The Ten Virgins, No Snoozing,
The Road Trip, Asleep At The Wheel, Staying Alert,
The Parable Of The Soils, The Working Mom, The Days Of Noah,
The Days Of Lot, Tiptoeing Around the Virgins, Don't Be Offensive.

LESSON 24 173

Holding Fast To The Word Of Life, The Pit, A Picture Of Our Salvation,
Grace And Faith, The Rope, An Interesting Experience, A Strange Sight,
Back On The Rope, On The Top.

LESSON 25 184

Keep Seeking The Things Above, Two Extremes, The Farmer,
One Last Issue, Keep Seeing The Things Above, Set Your Mind,
The Pleasures Of The Spirit, The Price Of Pleasure Is That We Sacrifice Joy,
Emotional Joys. The Secret Place Of The Most High, Gladness.

LESSON 26 194

Joys Of The Intellect, The Garden, What Do We Do Now?
Now For Planting, Weeding, Tending Our Thoughts, The Crown Prince,
The Doorway Of Difficulty, Knowledge Is Pleasant To The Soul,
Wait For the Seed To Come Up, The Hidden Springs Of God.

LESSON 27 206

Joys Of The Spirit, How Big Is God? God's Humor,
God's Intimacy, the Joy Of Compassion, The Joy Of Self-Mastery,
Conclusion.

THROUGH THE NARROW GATE

REVIVAL BEGINS WITH YOU!

"But his delight is in the law of the Lord, and in His law
*   he meditates day and night.*
And he will be like a tree firmly planted by streams of water,
*   which yields its fruit in its season,*
And its leaf does not wither and in whatever he does he prospers"
*   Psalm 1:2-3*

WHY AM I SO EMPTY?

What can possibly explain the waves of discontentment and emptiness that wash over us at the *best* of times? We allegedly live in the most prosperous and enlightened generation. The focus of all our attention and energy is self-fulfillment and yet the vast majority of people are neither happy nor satisfied with their lives. Self-fulfillment seems to be the one thing we lack! Of course everyone has bad days so we can easily explain the despair when our car breaks down on the way to work. What we can't explain is the lack of satisfaction that accompanies *getting the things we want*. We buy all the things that promise us excitement, we get the job that will be so rewarding, we move to the perfect neighborhood, our house is as good or better than our neighbor's, the coveted vehicle is sitting in our driveway, we spend all our time playing with the latest games and toys, but rather than having joy and contentment we are empty.

Why am I so empty? The answer to that question surprisingly starts way back in the book of Deuteronomy. Deuteronomy is part of the first five books of the Bible called the Books of the Law. They were written by God through Moses and form the foundation for the Jewish and Christian religions. Deuteronomy is the fifth and last book of the law and consists mainly of a summary of God's laws regarding man's conduct. In Deuteronomy chapter 28 we find distinct clues to the problem of mankind's state of general misery. As we begin reading this chapter, we find that Moses has just finished instructing his people at length about the 10 Commandments and the laws of God. He concludes with this foundation stone of our universe:

1

THE BLESSING

Now it shall be, if you will diligently obey the Lord your God, being careful to do all of His commandments which I command you today, the Lord your God will set you high above all the nations of the earth. And all these blessings shall come upon you and overtake you, if you will obey the Lord your God.

Blessed shall you be in the city, and blessed shall you be in the country. Blessed shall be the offspring of your body and the produce of your ground. Blessed shall be your basket and your kneading bowl [food provisions].

Blessed shall you be when you come in and when you go out. The Lord will cause your enemies who rise up against you to be defeated before you; they shall come out against you one way and flee before you seven ways.

The Lord will command the blessing upon you and on all you put your hand to. The Lord will establish you as a holy people to Himself as He swore to you, if you will keep the Commandments of the Lord your God and walk in His ways.

The Lord will make you abound in prosperity. The Lord will open for you His good storehouse, the heavens, to give rain to your land in its season and to bless all the work of your hand; and you shall lend to many but you shall not borrow.

And the Lord shall make you the head and not the tail if you will listen to the commandments of the Lord your God which I charge you today, to observe them carefully and do not turn aside from any of the words which I command you today, to the right or to the left.

THE CURSE

But it shall come about, if you will not obey the Lord your God, to observe to do all His commandments and His statutes, that all of these curses shall come upon you and overtake you;

Cursed shall you be in the city and cursed shall you be in the country. Cursed shall be your basket and your kneading bowl. Cursed shall be the offspring of your body and the produce of your ground.

Cursed shall you be when you come in, and cursed shall you be when you go out. The Lord will send upon you curses, confusion, and rebuke, in all you undertake to do.

The Lord will make the pestilence cling to you, the Lord will smite you with consumption [cancer] and with fever and with inflammation and with fiery heat and with the sword and with blight and with mildew and they shall pursue you until you perish.

The heaven which is over your head shall be bronze, and the earth iron. The Lord will make the rain powder and dust. The Lord will cause you to be defeated before your enemies; you shall go out one way against them, but flee seven ways before them, and you shall be an example of terror to all.

The Lord will smite you with boils and with tumors and with scab and with itch from which you cannot be healed. The Lord will smite you with madness and with blindness and with bewilderment of heart. You will only be oppressed and robbed continually. [NASB abbreviated]

Now we have some evidence of what the general problem is. To the question *"Why am I so empty?"* the Bible's answer is we have fallen on the wrong side of God's laws because of constantly ignoring them and breaking them.

And this is not peculiar to the Old Testament. The Apostle Paul says in the book of Colossians 3:25 *"For he who does wrong will receive the consequences of the wrong he has done and that without partiality."* That means no matter who you are or how justified you feel about doing something that God's Law says is wrong, you will be punished. Now let's start with the basics: Why are these laws so important to our personal happiness? Why can't we simply ignore them?

WHY IS LAW SO IMPORTANT?

We live in a time of great lawlessness. Laws are perceived as annoying, unnecessary and restricting to our personal freedom. If you are a believer you will hear over and over that you are 'under grace' not under the law. Any attempts to actually obey God's Word will be met with cries of

'legalism.' And so the law is perceived as bad and something to be avoided. We have even gone so far as to take great pride in openly disregarding laws. However, let's consider just one small example to help change our concept of the law.

How many times have you been irritated at being restrained by traffic laws? Now picture driving into one of our major cities. I will pick on Boston because it has a number of unusual intersections, some containing 5 or 6 convergent streets. During rush hour these intersections are considered chaotic. Each driver impatiently strains to get through, sometimes waiting two or three changes from red to green before successfully passing through. Irritation at being slowed down is evidenced on many faces. But this is not chaos. If there is a power outage and the traffic signals go down....now that's chaos!

Coincidently as these words were being written, the largest electric blackout in history occurred leaving NYC, Toronto, Detroit and a number of other cities with no power [I hope there's no connection!] The result of having no traffic signals was graphically displayed as the afternoon rush hour traffic came to a complete standstill. It became very evident that it is precisely *because* we have traffic laws that we can drive in the city at all. Without them confusion reigns and it is not even possible to drive through a crowded area. So traffic laws are not only good but essential for us to live and conduct business.

LESSON 2

THE BLESSING AND PENALTY OF THE LAW

Let's think a bit more about the importance of the law in our lives. Though we all complain about laws and how restrictive they are, yet if there were no law, it means you could be in your home and someone could walk in while you were watching TV, take your TV and leave!

Or, take your child! Or move into your house! And so it is *because* of the laws that we have some security. Law brings peace, order and safety to society. Without law there is anarchy. That means whoever is strongest takes what they want from the weaker. There is no protection and people live in complete fear. *So law itself is an instrument of God to bring*
security to all people. Remember that. However, as we examine this closely, we see it is not the law itself that keeps us in safety; it's because there is a system to *enforce* the law. So it's actually the *penalty* of the law that makes us safe in our homes. If there were no penalty, people would laugh at the law and then do whatever they wanted.

WITHOUT A PENALTY THERE IS NO LAW

Say an 'enlightened' governor made up a list of rules and regulations which would cause the citizens to live happily and prosperously with each other, then concluded by saying he dismissed the entire police force because he felt they were too intimidating. He was hoping his good constituents would willingly comply. He hoped they would obey. [Amazingly, this idea has become the essence of our modern child-raising techniques.] Of course, we all know what the results would be. Common sense tells us that the laws would be disregarded immediately. Why? Because human nature does not like to be restrained at all. Human nature will always take advantage of any leniency in order to get what it wants. However, when there is a real and meaningful penalty people are discouraged from breaking the law. They neither want to be fined nor jailed. Where there are strictly enforced, uniform penalties people are afraid to break the law and so the law holds up. Peace and security reign in the nation. Thus we can see that to have a penalty for breaking the law is absolutely necessary. *Without a penalty the law becomes merely a suggestion.*

OBEYING THE LAW BRINGS BLESSING
BREAKING THE LAW BRINGS PENALTY

Because of the penalty, those who ignore the law find life to be exceedingly miserable. They're constantly on edge, worried about the law, scared of punishment, or they've been caught and are being punished. However, those who keep the law find great benefits in being law-abiding. Those who obey the law find that rather than being restricted they actually have tremendous freedom. Those who can't resist the urge to speed in their car find themselves penalized. They want the freedom to go fast but instead they get their license suspended and can't even drive. For those who obey the law they have the ability to drive from coast to coast with no restriction, anytime of day or night, any destination - total freedom! With that in mind we go back to the original question once again *"Why am I so empty?"* Simply put, just as there are civil laws that govern our lives in our communities, there are spiritual laws set up by God to govern our behavior. If we break those laws, either civil or spiritual, we pay the price. Break the law and pay the price. Obey the law, enjoy your life.

THE PENALTY IS STRICT, BUT DELAYED

Most people don't even know that there are spiritual laws let alone keep them! And these laws are strictly enforced. There are serious consequences to breaking them. In our community there are police who enforce the law; if you break it you are notified immediately and pay the consequences. With God's laws there are no policemen per se there are only the penalties. Behavior that breaks His law automatically assigns a penalty to us. That penalty may be in the form of an outward punishment such as the open exposing of our hidden sins, it may be the loss of our marriage because of secret infidelity or most commonly it's the *resounding emptiness* that accompanies pushing away from God.

6

Hebrews 2: 2 says *"If the word of angels proved unalterable and every transgression and disobedience received a just recompense how shall we escape if we neglect so great a salvation."*

But as we read Deuteronomy 28 closely we see one little twist in God's enforcement system and that is the penalty does not come to  us instantly. No, it says they will come upon you and overtake you. In another version, it says they will pursue you and overtake you. So it's more like a penalty that is written out and stamped with our name on it and then mailed to us. If you speed while driving you will not be penalized on the spot, rather you will receive a summons in the mail a month later and then you will pay the fine. There is a delay. On your first speeding offense you are tempted to think that you got away with it, but sooner or later that fine will come to you with a legal notice informing you to pay up or take the consequences. It is just the same with God's laws. There is a delay, but the penalty will pursue us and overtake us. *"All these curses shall come upon you and overtake you."* Every single time we do something against God's law a penalty is assigned to us, then it is sealed and sent with our name on it. Ecclesiastes 8:11 says, *"The sentence against an evil deed is not executed quickly, therefore the hearts of the sons of men among them are given fully to evil."* Why are we so empty? We've broken God's laws for a long time and the penalties have caught up with us! So we are empty, unfulfilled, hopeless, afraid and in despair because we are reaping the consequences of breaking laws that we didn't even know existed!

GOD'S LAWS ARE RADIOACTIVE!

If you think that isn't fair consider this. Those who first began working in the nuclear field did not have any understanding of the laws of radiation. As a consequence, they were exposed to something completely invisible and undetected. Over time, because of their ignorance of those laws of physics, they developed deadly diseases. In the same way when we break

God's laws we develop deadly diseases. And just like it was greatly in their favor to learn the laws of radiation, so it is our best possible good to learn what God's laws are so we can start to escape the results of breaking them.

GOD'S LAWS GOVERN THE HEART

The laws of God differ from the laws of our communities in this respect - our civil laws govern outward behavior while God's laws govern our inward behavior as well. The civil law prevents us only from stealing, God's law prevents us from *wanting* to steal. The civil law steps in to prevent us from murdering, God's law steps in to prevent us from even being angry with someone. So, you can be perfectly law-abiding in terms of the civil government, not stealing, not killing etc. and at the same time you can be breaking God's laws *all day long*. Every time we are jealous, or spiteful, or angry, or selfish, or arrogant, or rude, or lustful, or proud, or vain, we are breaking God's laws which govern our heart attitudes! Then, every time we break a law of God we receive a stamped penalty addressed to us! The penalty pursues us and overtakes us no matter where we are or what we're doing. We think for a time that we are getting away with it, but it is not possible to escape the consequences of breaking God's laws. And remember from Colossians 3:25 that it doesn't matter who we are or who we think we are, God's law is impartial. This makes us very anxious to find out what the laws are so we can escape the penalty. But that puts us into an even greater dilemma!

LEARNING ABOUT THE PENALTY OF THE LAW
DOES NOT STOP US FROM BREAKING IT

Unfortunately, just discovering that there are spiritual laws and heavy penalties does not stop us from breaking them. What's the problem? In two words - sin nature. We have a natural predisposition to do what is wrong. In common language we love to sin. It's as natural to us as breathing.

We take great delight in criticizing people!

We love to feel we're better than someone else!

We want people to be envious of us!

We're glad when people give in to our demands!

We love being lazy!

We want to do what we want to do!

We love to party!

We can't wait to get the newest thing so we can show it off!

It feels good to blast the one who irritates you!

Belittling people is second nature to us!

We hate anything that takes us away from our pleasures!

We loathe anything that infringes on us having a good time!

We continue to break the law even though we're scared of punishment because we can't stop ourselves. We naturally and automatically do all those things which bring penalty. We are proud, we are lustful, we are selfish and *we love being that way!*

"Then the Lord saw the wickedness of man was great on the earth, and that every intent of the thoughts of his heart was only evil continually." Gen 6:5. What do we do?

ENTER JESUS

Jesus is God's miracle to save our lives.

Jesus, God's own son, in His tender mercy and compassion came to earth as a man, uniting Himself with the human race. As a man he took the full penalty that we, the human race, deserved because of breaking God's laws. When we were condemned, He took the death penalty *in our place* by being crucified on a cross. By his atonement, of shedding his blood on our behalf, we are pardoned if we turn to God with sincere repentance, trusting in him to save us! That was God's amazing plan for our redemption. But, there are actually *two* specific reasons that Jesus came to Earth. The first was to cause the penalty of the law to be lifted from us by taking the penalty Himself. In terms of civil government, He caused the charges against us to be dropped. The second was to bring about a change of heart within us so that we no longer *desire* to break the law. Both are essential. Let's explain.

9

The first reason is self-evident. In order to rescue His people He had to release them from the punishment of the law. This is as simple as understanding a Presidential pardon. Before a President of the U.S. leaves office he has the power to issue pardons to anyone, regardless of the crime they have committed. He signs the certificate and they are free - even if they are convicted felons! Jesus obtained a certificate of pardon from God the Father for all those who were guilty under the law regardless of the crime, by personally taking the full punishment for our sins by His death on the cross! This pardon was granted to all who personally come to God through faith in His Son, Jesus.

The second reason, that He came to bring a change of heart. This

is best explained by the following illustration: If a governor decided to show mercy to convicted felons in the state penitentiary and issued a full pardon to all the inmates, what would you have? You'ld have several hundred happy convicted felons running around loose on the streets. They would still be criminals, and they would be getting the opportunity to break more laws. They would be exactly the same people and the net effect of the pardon would be to make them feel they had gotten away with their crimes. So it would actually make them bolder in their disregard for the law. If Jesus simply granted us pardon, we would be no better off than we were before, because like most convicted felons, we would use our freedom to go out and commit more crimes!

For the pardon to have lasting effect we would also have to be reformed. We would have to become changed people that *wanted* to do what was right. We would have to have a change of heart. That is exactly what Jesus came to do. After sacrificing Himself on our behalf so we could go free, He then provided for the Holy Spirit to be poured out so that men and women everywhere could have a brand new love for God and a desire to obey Him. Deuteronomy 30:6 says *"The Lord your God will circumcise your heart to love the Lord your God with all your heart and with all your soul, in order that you may live" and Deut. 30:8 "You shall again obey the Lord and observe all His commandments." Hebrews 10:16-17 says "This is the covenant that I will make with them, after those days I will put My laws upon their heart, and upon their heart I will write them.... And their sins and their lawless deeds I will remember no more".*

JESUS STOPS THE CYCLE OF SIN AND DEATH

As mentioned, it is not possible for us to stop our natural inclination to break God's laws. We are weak and we desire to sin. So the thing we desire also causes our misery and destruction! Sin is like doing drugs. Once we taste it we are irresistibly drawn to it. All the while it is killing us. Jesus stops the cycle of sin and death by first forgiving us, and then by giving us a desire to be good. We love to obey because we love Him. He enters our life and gives us a brand new heart. Once we receive Christ as our Savior by faith we are forgiven, then we are slowly cleansed from our actual sins. As we begin living in obedience we start to see the amazing blessings of God pour over us. We begin to be pursued and overtaken by the blessings of God!

"He who has My commandments and keeps them, he it is who
loves me: and he who loves me shall be loved by my Father,
And I will love him and reveal Myself to him" [John 14:21].
"If we confess our sins He is faithful and righteous to forgive us
our sins and to cleanse us from all unrighteousness." 1John 1:9

11

LESSON 3

SO WHAT ARE GOD'S LAWS?

In the last chapter we established that God has set up spiritual laws, that there are penalties for breaking the laws and blessings for keeping them. By God's divine enforcement system the penalties for breaking the laws are automatically sent to us. They pursue us and overtake us. No matter where we go those penalties are forwarded to us. *Whether you believe in God and His laws or not makes absolutely no difference. These laws exist!* It is very important for us to learn what God's laws are so that we do not stumble and break them, because the penalty of the law is *harsh* and makes our lives miserable.

On the other side, the blessing of the Lord for obedience is also sent to us. The blessings also pursue us and overtake us. The reward for keeping the law is wonderful, not like regular earthly law. With earthly law the blessing for obedience is in *not* being punished. Simply, if you're good, nothing bad happens. Not so with God's law! King David says it well in Psalm 19;

" *The law of the Lord is perfect, restoring the soul. The testimony*
    of the Lord is sure, making wise the simple.
The precepts of the Lord are right, rejoicing the heart.
The commandment of the Lord is pure enlightening the eye.
The fear of the Lord is clean, enduring forever.
They are more desirable than gold, yes, than much fine gold.
Sweeter also than honey and the drippings of the honeycomb.
In keeping them there is great reward."

Now, the question is *what* law was David referring to when he said keeping them was sweeter than the honeycomb? Since he lived approximately 1000 BC we know he wasn't speaking of anything from the New Testament. He also wasn't referring to the sacrificial laws outlined in the book of Leviticus, which make up the bulk of Jewish worship, because he says later in Psalm 40, *"Sacrifice and meal offering You have not desired; My ears You have opened; Burnt offering and sin offering You have not required. I delight to do Thy will O my God; Thy law is within my heart" [Ps. 40; 6, 8].* So the law David is referring to is the 10 Commandments and the other laws regarding treating people kindly and avoiding sin.

The 10 Commandments have become increasingly unpopular in recent years because they seem too restrictive for our modern lifestyle. In fact, most people have never read them and don't know what they are. As an example, see how many you can remember without reading them.... because of that we will list them now in order.

THE 10 COMMANDMENTS

You shall have no other gods before Me.

You shall not make for yourself an idol, or any likeness of what is in heaven above or on the earth beneath or in the waters under the earth. You shall not worship them or serve them; for I the Lord your God am a jealous God, visiting the iniquity of the fathers on the children, on the third and fourth generations of those who hate Me, but showing lovingkindness to thousands, to those who love Me and keep My commandments.

You shall not take the name of the Lord your God in vain, for the Lord will not leave him unpunished who takes His name in vain.

Remember the sabbath day, to keep it holy. Six days you shall labor and do all your work but the seventh day is a sabbath of the Lord your God; in it you shall not do any work, you or your son or your daughter, your male or your female servant or your cattle or your sojourner who stays with you. For in six days the Lord made the heavens and the earth, the sea and all that is in them, and rested on the seventh day; therefore the Lord blessed the sabbath day and made it holy.

Honor your father and mother that your days may be prolonged in the land which the Lord your God gives you.

You shall not murder.

You shall not commit adultery.

You shall not steal.

You shall not bear false witness against your neighbor.

You shall not covet [desire] your neighbor's house; You shall not covet your neighbor's wife or anything that belongs to your neighber.   NASB Exodus 20: 3-17 [abbreviated]

13

These same Commandments are re-examined in the New Testament by Jesus who explains them carefully in the Sermon on the Mount [Matthew 5-7]. In this powerful passage of scripture, Jesus explains the inner meaning of the laws and shows that God goes far beyond the laws themselves to the heart attitude behind the laws. God is not content that we don't murder someone, He does not even want strong anger against anyone. He is concerned that our heart is pure.

THE FIRST AND SECOND COMMANDMENTS
ALONE EXPLAIN OUR CONDITION

To give an example of how the Commandments affect us personally we will now examine the first laws of God as revealed in the 10 Commandments: *I am the Lord your God, you shall have no other gods before Me. You shall not make for yourself an idol [Ex. 20; 3-4a].* These commandments and the breaking of these far-reaching laws are actually the *primary* cause of our misery. Most people of our time and culture dismiss these commandments as not relevant to our society. They reason that since they're not sacrificing to any pagan idols, they have these laws pretty well wrapped up. Not so! These verses are clarified in Deuteronomy 6:5. *"And you shall love the Lord your God with all your heart and with all your soul and with all your might."* The essence of these laws is that there should be nothing in our life we love more than God. When we consider them in this light, we can see them touching every area of our life. To put it bluntly, we have false gods before Him all day long. In fact, except in rare cases, *all* we have are false gods! Beginning when we are born into this world, we cram our lives full with every false god imaginable. The work of salvation is the process of coming to know the true God and getting rid of all the others. Let's explain.

FALSE GODS

A false god is anything in our lives we look to for joy, happiness or meaning apart from Jesus. Anything we look to apart from the true God is a false god. That means if we look to all the passions of the flesh, they are idols. If we take our pleasure from drinking, drugs, rock n' roll and lust, those are our false gods. They have taken the

14

 place of the real God in our lives. If we look to TV, music, sports, dancing, movies, entertainment, and computer games for our joy those are false gods. If we look to shopping or cars or new things for our pleasure, they are all false gods. If we look to boyfriends or girlfriends or husbands or wives for our joy, they become false idols. If we look to money or success or investments, they become pagan gods. Everything striven for as a source of our fulfilment separate from the real God is a false god and makes us liable for punishment. Are all these things wrong? Isn't that going too far? No, some are not wrong at all in themselves [such as husbands and wives!]. The key is that we are looking to them instead of Jesus for our joy. We seek after them for pleasure and meaning instead of seeking God.

AND WHAT IS THE PUNISHMENT?

The punishment for violating the first commandments is twofold: First, there is the universal law built into the reality of human experience. If we look to anything for happiness without God being in it, it will disappoint us and let us down - hard. Second, there is the actual punishment which will pursue us and overtake us. The full penalty of the law will eventually be demanded of us. Part of it will come to us now in our earthly life; the rest will be revealed at the Great Judgment Day. In the first punishment we see the truth in our axiom 'break the law and pay the price; obey the law, enjoy your life.' Our whole life becomes a series of complete disappointments and frustrations because everthing we look to for joy and pleasure apart from Jesus lets us down.
- The boyfriend walks away. The husband is unfaithful. The car gets scratched and dented.
-The stock market crashes. Video games leave us empty and depressed. Our team loses.
-Drugs and alcohol leave us dead.
-Sex outside marriage leaves us with offspring, disease and no one to help raise the children.
- The perfect job has irritating co-workers.

15

- The perfect neighborhood is made up of people just like us who are only concerned about ourselves!

In fact, this let down is so universal that these commandments alone answer our question of why we are so empty. If we examine our

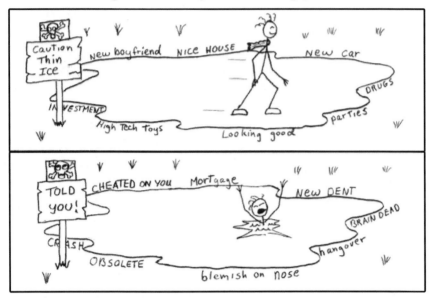

emptiness, we will find without exception that it is because we were looking at some earthly happiness that ended up disappointing us. When we're miserable many times it's because we are in fact, breaking the first commandments. We have set up some false god, some source of happiness, and it has let us down. We pay a severe price for having false gods. Our world falls apart. So, first we have the built in penalty of trusting something that can't be trusted, second we have the actual punishment and curse for breaking the law - the punishment that is sent to us and overtakes us. So we have the built-in punishment of all these things letting us down, then we have the penalty of the law added to it, thus we have the source of our misery and emptiness.

Law: To whatever degree we look to things other than God for our happiness, that is the degree of misery we have.

IT IS GOD TRYING TO SAVE OUR LIVES

Now isn't that kind of mean? Isn't God being too harsh, too strict? How harsh is a mother who strictly enforces a rule for her kids not to play in the street? Is that harsh? Is she doing it to be mean? Because she doesn't want her children to have any fun? No, of course not. She does it to protect the child's life. She loves the child more than anyone else in the world and doesn't want anything bad to happen to him. In the same way, our true Heavenly Father also doesn't want anything bad to happen to us. Every time we pursue a false god of any sort, we get hurt - not just hurt, but actually threatened with death, like playing in the street. But it's not just death, it's eternal death, *dead forever*. God, the true loving parent doesn't want any of His precious children to be dead forever. That doesn't sound harsh at all, does it? As we turn to 1 John, chapter 2: 15-17 we see that God is protecting us.

"Do not love the world, nor the things in the world. If anyone loves the world, the love of the Father is not in him. For all that is in the world, the lust of the flesh, the lust of the eyes, and the boastful pride of life is not from the Father, but is from the world. And the world is passing away and also its lusts; but the one who does the will of God abides forever."

Why do bad things happen to good people? Simple. It is God trying to save their lives. He's trying to get them to let go of the things that are perishing to hold onto the One who will remain.

OUR FALSE GODS WILL LEAD US TO A TRUE HELL

If we base our lives on the things of this world, the world is passing away and all those things that we live for are passing with it! We will go to a place where there are no passions, or rather, no fulfillment of passions. In hell there will be only the burning desire for all those things, but those things won't exist! Hell will be like a drug addict locked up in jail with no drugs. Remember that. Heaven is a place where God has taken away the passions for evil and prepared the fulfillment of every good and lawful desire. Therefore His people will live in perfect delight and contentment.

Every single decision we make and everything we do sets us up for one or the other. If we ignore the First and Second Commandments we prepare ourselves for burning flames of passion in hell. If we become afraid and begin to seek God earnestly, He will rescue us cleanse us from evil and evil desires.

LESSON 4

CHRISTIANITY, THE RELIGION OF GRACE

Now that we have firmly established we are in serious trouble, we can start to understand the 'Good News' which the gospel of Jesus represents. There is a specific order to God's revelation to man and it is for a purpose. The purpose is this: God first sent the LAW, meaning the 10 Commandments, in order to cause men everywhere to understand their sin. He established the law that their sin might be defined. It is very similar to a parent correcting a little child. In nearly every case the child will excuse himself by saying 'I didn't know' or 'you never told me.' We are all notorious for making up excuses for our bad behavior. The Law, the 10 Commandments, once and for all time, tells us exactly what God expects of us. There are no more gray areas. When that was accomplished, He sent His Son to be our Savior, to save us from our sins. The Apostle Paul says, *"Therefore the law has become our tutor to lead us to Christ that we may be justified by faith."* This second part is what distinguishes Christianity from every other religion of the world. Christianity is a religion of grace.

RELIGION OF WORKS

All other religions of the world are based on *works*. That means a code of behavior is established and those who live up to the standard go to a heaven-like place when they die [or after a series of deaths and reincarnations]. Those who are interested in going to the heaven-like place begin a rigorous lifestyle of trying to obey the religion. Hence it is called a *religion of works*. It is based on how well they perform or live up to the religious code. They go to temples, 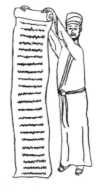 they offer sacrifices, they go door to door, they blow themselves up, they adhere to severe bodily regimens - all for the purpose of attaining approval in order to go to heaven. Those who don't understand

Christianity also try to use it in the same way. They try to measure how good they are by how closely they follow the rules. Each church has it's own set of rules and regulations and the measure of whether they are approved or 'saved' is based upon how well they live up to the church's expectations. When they do that they turn Christianity into a false religion. Right now, as you are discovering the effects of breaking the law, your first impulse will normally be to start trying hard to be good. But here's another twist!

CHRISTIANITY IS NOT BASED ON
HOW WELL WE KEEP THE LAWS OF GOD

The Bible does *not* say that if we keep so many laws so much of the time, we'll go to heaven. Christianity is a *religion of grace* and that means our salvation is not based on how well we do keeping the laws of God. That's a good thing. Why? Because we would all be convicted and hung! Think how many times in one day we break the First Commandment alone. So if it were up to us and our ability to be good, none of us could make it. That's precisely what the Bible does say.

The book of Romans 3:10-12 says,

> *"There is none righteous, not even one; There is none*
> *who understand, There is none who seeks for God.*
> *All have turned aside, together they have become useless;*
> *There is none who does good, there is not even one."*

Romans 3:23 says,

> *"For all have sinned and fall short of the glory of God."*

Then it goes on to say, Romans 6:23,

> *"The wages of sin is death, but the free gift of God is*
> *eternal life in Christ Jesus our Lord."*

With these words we can clearly see that if Christianity were a religion of works all of us would be condemned! That's because we *are* all condemned. We break God's laws from morning to night in ways we don't even know. We sin continually in our thoughts and actions. Even the few good things we do are polluted with impure motives of wanting to be recognized.

SIN SEPARATES US FROM GOD

God is life. He is the fountain of life and He is the source of all true life and happiness. In Him is joy, peace and fulfilment.

Psalm 36:8-9 says;
> *"They drink their fill of the abundance of Thy house and*
> *Thou dost give them to drink of the River of Thy Delights.*
> *For with Thee is the Fountain of Life and*
> *In Thy light we see light."*

Psalm 34:8-10 says,
> *"O taste and see that the Lord is good.*
> *How blessed is the man who takes refuge in Him!*
> *O fear the Lord you His saints;*
> *For to those who fear Him there is no want.*
> *The young lions do lack and suffer hunger;*
> *But those who seek the Lord shall not be*
> *In want of any good thing."*

When we sin we push ourselves further and further away from Him. Since He is the very essence of life, we are automatically separated from all that is pleasing, rewarding, joyful and satisfying. That leaves us very empty. Then, because we feel so terrible, what do we do? We go out and sin harder and more than before in a desperate attempt to make life seem exciting again. Of course, that makes us receive more penalties which makes us feel even worse. So our lives get drier and drier.

THE QUICKSAND EFFECT

As you begin to find out what God's laws are and then find out there are huge blessings attached to obeying them, you naturally want to start obeying so you can get out of the trouble you're in. But, unfortunately we are like people who are in a pit of quicksand - not just any quicksand, we are struggling in the *Quicksand of Death*. We are dying and will drown if we aren't rescued!

Then someone calls to you from the shore and tells you that there is safe, solid ground just a short distance away. As you look, you can see people, who have been rescued from the same pit, walking around safe and happy. The solid ground is God's Word, God's salvation, God's protection and blessing on your life. When you see it you have an automatic reaction of struggling to get there. You are frightened of drowning and want to get to safety. So you struggle to be good, but as you make determined resolutions you find it's to no avail. You keep going back to your bad habits. Unfortunately that's the nature of  quicksand, the harder you struggle the deeper you sink. The Quicksand of Death is your sins. Your sins are pulling you down to eternal death and no matter how you struggle you can't save yourself!

You are condemned by your sins and you can't stop sinning even if you want to. Even those who struggle to be good can't reach safe ground. So you do the only thing you can do - cry out for help.

JESUS HIMSELF REACHES OUT TO US

As you reach the point of utter despair, as the emptiness of your life makes your world devoid of meaning, as you find you're simply going through the motions of living but there is no joy, call out to God. As you humble yourself before God and turn to Him for help a surprising thing happens! Jesus will come right down to the pit and offer to pull you to safety. As you take hold of His strong arm through repentance and trust He will begin to lift you right up out of the quicksand. By holding onto Him by faith you will actually be rescued! He will pull you out and set you on firm ground. Where you would have only perished in your sins and the punishment of the Law, God through Jesus, reaches out to you and says 'I'll pull you to safety.' All the religions of the world cannot do that one act which God does. He does something totally beyond our ability and rescues us when we have no way to keep from perishing. He saves us without regard for the fact that it was our own willful disobedience that got us into the quicksand in the first place. He rescues us as though we were His own lost brother or sister about to drown.

When Jesus took our punishment by dying in our place it gave Him the authority to rescue those who are drowning in sin.

That's why people who have been saved love Jesus so much. He is their rescuer, He is their lifeline. They would be dead if it weren't for Him. In fact they couldn't even reach out or hold on to Him if it weren't for His supernatural touch giving them strength. Even the strength is a gift from God. The Bible says *"For by grace you have been saved through faith, and that not of ourselves, it is the gift of God, not of works, lest anyone should boast." Eph. 2:8.*

In a recent issue of a popular magazine the back cover showed a man unabashedly embracing another man. As you read the story you found that one man had just saved the other from certain death. There was an unashamed bond between them. The rescued man was proud to be seen embracing his rescuer by millions of people. In the same way, we who have been rescued by Jesus have an unashamed love and gratitude toward Him. He is our Savior.

LESSON 5

JESUS' SALVATION

Let's sum up our last lesson. Willfully or ignorantly we break all sorts of God's laws. We begin to reap the penalty of the law and so begin to sink in the Quicksand of Death because of our sins. Someone points out that there is a place of safety; that is, we find that if we obey God, great blessings will come upon us instead of great curses. So we begin to struggle to get there. We try to start being good and find we can't. We are so weak that despite all our good intentions, we run to sin. We love everything that kills us. Finally, after we sink deeper and deeper into trouble, we realize that unless there is a miracle, we are dead. We call out to God for help, then Jesus comes to rescue us. He is our miracle. He reaches out and says, "I'll pull you to safety." This required that Jesus first take the penalty of the law for us by dying on the cross in our place as though He were us. It was necessary for Him to do that in order to fulfill the requirements of the law. Why? Remember back to the previous chapter? Someone had to take the punishment. If there were no penalty enforced there would be no law. It would fall apart and we would have the 10 Suggestions.

And what is the salvation that Jesus has brought to us? First, as we discussed earlier, He causes the death penalty charged against us to be dropped. He brings us forgiveness for all our sins so we do not have to receive the just penalty for our crimes. Second, He plants in us a new desire to be good so that we do not simply use our new freedom to go out and sin again. He gives us pardon and begins to change our heart to want to become obedient children. What follows from there are the Blessings of Obedience found in Dueteronomy 28.

HOW CAN I GET SAVED?

Now that we understand the importance of being 'saved' or more accurately, 'rescued,' how do we go about it? What is the actual process of coming to peace with God? This is the most important question of your entire eternal life. For those who have met our Loving Savior already you can use this as a guide to help lead others to a personal relationship with Christ.

SIN IS THE ISSUE

Jesus came to save us from sin. Remember sin is what brings the curse of God. The Quicksand of Death is made up of every sinful thought and action we have. Sin is the issue.

Matt. 1:21 "And she will bear a Son; and you shall call His name Jesus, for it is He who will save His people from their sins."

1John 3:4, 5a "Everyone who practices sin practices lawlessness and sin is lawlessness. And you know that He appeared in order to take away sins."

Rom. 6:23 "For the wages of sin is death, but the free gift of God is eternal life in Christ Jesus our Lord."

ADMIT IN YOUR HEART THAT YOU ARE A SINNER

Rom. 1:8 "For the wrath of God is revealed from heaven against all ungodliness and unrighteousness of men."

Rom. 3:23 "For all have sinned and fall short of the glory of God."

ADMIT YOUR NEED FOR A SAVIOR

TITUS 3:5 "He saved us not on the basis of deeds that we have done in righteousness but according to His mercy by the washing of regeneration and the renewing by the Holy Spirit."

1Peter 2:24 "He Himself bore our sins in His body on the cross, that we might die to sin and live to righteousness; for by His wounds you were healed."

Rom. 5:8 "But God demonstrates His own love towards us in that while we were yet sinners Christ died for us."

CONFESS YOUR SINS

1John 1:9 "If we confess our sins He is faithful and righteous to forgive us and cleanse us from all unrighteousness."

Luke 24:46, 47 "Thus it is written that the Christ should suffer and rise from the dead the third day and repentance for forgiveness of sins should be proclaimed in His name to all nations."

ASK HIM TO SAVE YOU

Rom. 10:13 "Whoever will call upon the name of the Lord will be saved."

John 6:35 "I am the bread of life, he who comes to me shall not hunger and he who believes in Me shall never thirst."

John 6:37b "And the one who comes to Me I will certainly not cast out."

John 1:12 "But as many as received Him, to them He gave the right to become children of God, even to those who believe in His name."

BELIEVE IN YOUR HEART

Heb. 11:6 "Without faith it is impossible to please Him, for he who comes to God must believe that He is and that He is a rewarder of those who seek him."

John 3:16-18 "For God so loved the world that He gave His only begotten Son, that whoever believes in him should not perish but have eternal life. For God did not send the Son into the world to judge the world, but that the world should be saved through Him. He who believes in him is not judged; he who does not believe has been judged already, because he has not believed in the name of the only begotten son of God."

2 Tim. 1:9 "Who has saved us and called us with a holy calling not according to our works but according to His own purpose and grace which was granted us in Christ Jesus from all eternity."

John 5:24 "Truly, truly I say to you, he who hears My word and believes in Him who sent Me has eternal life and does not come into judgement, but has passed out of death into life."

John 8:12 "I am the light of the world; he who follows Me shall not walk in darkness but shall have the light of life."

CONFESS WITH YOUR MOUTH

Matt. 10:32 "Everyone therefore who confesses Me before men, I will also confess him before My Father who is in heaven."

Rom. 10:9 - 11 "If you confess with your mouth Jesus as Lord and believe in your heart that God raised him from the dead, you shall be saved, for with the heart man believes resulting in righteousness and with his mouth he confesses resulting in salvation. Whoever believes in Him will not be disappointed."

RECEIVE IT BY FAITH

John 10:28, 29 "And I give eternal life to them, and they shall never perish; and no one shall snatch them out of My hand. My Father who has given them to Me is greater than all; and no one is able to snatch them out of the Father's hand."

Rom. 8:1 "There is therefore now no condemnation for those who are in Christ Jesus."

John 11:25 "I am the resurrection and the life; he who believes in Me shall live even if he dies."

BE BAPTIZED

Mark 16:16 "He who has believed and been baptized shall be saved. But he who has disbelieved shall be condemned."

Rom. 6:4 "Therefore we have been buried with him through baptism into death in order that as Christ was raised from the dead through the glory of the Father, so we too might walk in fullness of life."

Matt. 28:19-20 "Go therefore and make disciples of all nations, baptizing them in the name of the Father and the Son and the Holy Spirit, teaching them to observe all that I commanded you."

BE PUTTING TO DEATH THE DEEDS OF SIN

As evidence that you have truly been born again you will begin to display a transformed life.

Rom. 8:13 "For if you live according to the flesh you must die; but if by the Spirit you are putting to death the deeds of the body you will live."

Rom. 12:2a "Do not be conformed to the world but be transformed by the renewing of your mind."

John 3:36a "He who believes in the Son has eternal life but he who does not obey will not see life, but the wrath of God abides on him."

1Peter 2:11 "Beloved I urge you as aliens and strangers to abstain from earthly lusts which wage war against your soul."

Col. 3:5-8 "Consider the members of your earthly body as dead to immorality, impurity, passion, evil desire and greed which amounts to idolatry. For it is on account of these things that the wrath of God will come and in them you once walked, when you were living in them. But now you also put them all aside; anger, wrath, malice, slander and abusive speech from your mouth."

1John 2:15 "Do not love the world or the things of the world. If anyone loves the world the love of the Father is not in him."

JUST TALK TO GOD

This all sounds complicated at first, but it is actually very simple. In fact, we often make it more difficult than it really is. The way to approach God for the salvation of your soul is just this - talk to God. Go to Him privately or with a Christian friend and tell Him you would like to become His child. Tell Him of all your struggles. Openly confess your doubts to Him. Ask Him to show you that He is really there. You will be surprised by what happens! Then confess your sins to Him. Take your time and really get all the burdens off your soul. Then ask Jesus to come into your heart and make it new......and He will!

Then begin to exercise your faith. The Bible says to believe in your heart and confess with your mouth that Jesus is Lord and you will be saved. Begin to thank God for your new life with Him. Begin to thank Him that He loves you and has heard your prayers. Thank Him that He has forgiven all your sins. This is *faith* in action. This is how you take hold of His hand so He can pull you out of the quicksand of death. You may or may not feel any different right then, but God has made you His child! Keep rejoicing in Him and soon you will be overwhelmed by the sweet presence of God!

HOW TO PRAY

Here is an example of how to pray:

'Dear Lord Jesus, I freely confess to you all my sins. I am tired of reaping the consequences of sin. I will die in my sins if you don't rescue me. Please forgive me for every wrong thing I have ever done [elaborate here] and cleanse me from them. I need you Lord Jesus and pray that You will come to me and make Your home in my heart. I give You my life. I pray that You would make me a new person. I thank you that You have said anyone who comes to You, You will in no way cast out.

I believe that You love me and even now have received me as Your child. Thank you for forgiving my sins. Thank you for accepting me and making me Your child this day. Lord, I receive Your Holy Spirit to make me a good and obedient child. Amen.'

There is one more point to be made while we are on the quicksand illustration: We could be sinking in the quicksand, someone could be holding his arm right over us all day long, and still we could drown in the quicksand. Why? Because we didn't take hold of his arm. Jesus could be reaching His arm out to you, personally, right now but you will still perish if you don't grab hold of it. When we do take hold we begin to be rescued. And what does that mean? How do we grab hold of His arm?

His arm being extended to us is *grace,* us grabbing hold of it is *faith. By grace you have been saved through faith [Eph. 2:8].* And what is faith? It is another word for belief. So if we believe God we will be saved. But what are we supposed to believe? We are to believe the Word of God. We have just listed many verses of the Bible concerning the issue of your salvation. While they remain words on a page they will have no effect on your soul. The words become alive and able to rescue us as we believe them. Believing is our active participation in the process of being rescued. Believing God's Word does not come naturally or easily to us. It requires work! Our minds are natually inclined to doubt and turn from the truth so we must fight to believe that God's word to us is true. We should repeat His good promises to us out loud. We must begin to thank Him for all the things His word promises. Thanking Him is the single most effective way of demonstrating faith. Here's an example:

You've read all the preceeding scripture verses and have prayed to Him that He would forgive your sins and make you a new person in Christ. Immediately after, you find yourself doubting that anything happened - that you were just praying to the air! Your enemy, the devil, will do anything to stop you from growing close to Christ and doubt is his most effective weapon. But in fact as you prayed God accepted you and you were born again. Begin to thank God for your salvation! Begin to rejoice that His words are true. Treat it as a matter of fact that you are now a child of God! That active faith is your holding on to His outstretched arm of grace which He has extended to you. If you continue to believe you will be overwhelmed by God's blessing! God will reward your faith, and joy and peace will fill your heart.

LESSON 6

THE TRANSITION OF THE LAW

As you look ahead now you will see more chapters covering the 10 Commandments. Since we just learned that we are saved by grace and not by works [that is by diligently following the commandments], why are we now studying the 10 Commandments? Good question! Now that we have received Christ as our Savior the Law takes on a brand new meaning.

TWO MEANINGS OF LAW

The first thing we must do is examine the word Law as used in the Bible. It is used in two different ways to mean two different things.

One meaning of the word Law refers to the 10 Commandments and the various laws governing man's moral behavior. 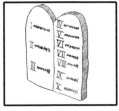 These are called the *Moral Law*. We see this clearly in Psalm 19 where David speaks of the delights of God's laws. He says, " *The Law of the Lord is perfect restoring the soul, the precepts of the Lord are right rejoicing the heart. In keeping them there is great reward."*

The second meaning refers to the system of sacrificial offerings set up by God for the temporary covering of sin. This *Ceremonial Law* prescribed exact procedures for offering acceptable sacrifices to God. They could be performed only by the Levites or  priests of God. This use of the word Law is seen clearly in Hebrews 7:8 *"For the Law appoints men as high priests who are weak." And in Heb. 10: 1-3 "For the Law since it has only a shadow of the good things to come and not the very form of things, can never by the same sacrifices year by year, which they offer continually, make perfect those who draw near. Otherwise would they not cease to be offered, because the worshippers, having once been cleansed, would no longer have had a consciousness of sin. But in those sacrifices there is a reminder of sin year by year."*

THE CEREMONIAL LAW WAS REPLACED
BY THE COMING OF JESUS

Jesus abolished the Ceremonial Law by His coming, which is explained carefully in Hebrews 10:4-10;

"For it is impossible for the blood of bulls and goats to take away
sins. Therefore when He comes into the world He says;
"Sacrifice and sin offering you have not desired, but a body Thou
hast prepared for Me. In whole burnt offerings and sacrifices
for sin Thou hast taken no pleasure."
Then I said, "Behold I have come [in the roll of the Book it is
written of Me] to do Thy will, O God."
Then He said, "I have come to do Thy will." He takes away the
first in order to establish the second.
By this will we have been sanctified through the offering of the
body of Jesus Christ once for all."

He takes away this Law, that is the Ceremonial or Sacrificial Law in order to establish another, which is the Law of Grace. This is a self-evident truth. The Ceremonial Law prescribed yearly sacrifices for sin which had to be offered over and over again. But when the true sacrifice came, that is the Spotless Lamb of God, those temporary sacrifices were finished. To continue sacrificing after Jesus' death was equivalent to insisting on paying installments on a loan that had already been paid off in full. It was senseless and unnecessary. Those who continued to offer sacrifices were in effect

telling God over and over that they did not accept the atonement provided by Jesus' death. It was very offensive to God and was the very reason He caused the temple where the sacrifices were offered to be torn down and never rebuilt. So when the Bible speaks of the Law coming to an end, it is the *Ceremonial Law* of sacrifices it is referring to. This is what Paul the Apostle meant when he addresses this in Romans 7: 6,

"But now we have been released from the law,
having died to that by which we were bound, so that we serve in
the newness of the Spirit, not in the oldness of the letter."

He is saying that we are no longer under their old system of pre-scribed rituals and diets which the religious leaders had made central to their Old Covenant observances. We must remember, too, that Paul was always wrestling with Jewish leaders who were persecuting him. Paul himself was a Jewish leader and all his arguments about the Law being abolished referred to a twisted religion of works based on out-ward ceremonies. Jesus also raised a whip against these same scribes, lawyers and Pharisees.

THERE IS ALSO A CHANGE IN THE OTHER LAW

Now, regarding the other meaning of the Law, the Moral Law, which is the 10 Commandments, we also have a change. It is a common assumption in modern days to lump the Law [10 Commandments] in with the Law [Ceremonial] and throw them both out. Since Christians know that they are no longer under the *law* but under *grace* they often abandon everything to do with law. This becomes a snare and a source of great error in the modern church which leads to all types of sin and confusion. The Moral Law [10 Commandments] is not annulled with the Ceremonial Law, however a change does take place which alters it's character. This is one of the central concepts of the Reformation which so powerfully impacted the world.

The transition that takes place in the Law [10 commandments] under the New Covenant is this: We are no longer under the *curse* of the law. Galations 3;13 says it perfectly,

"Christ redeemed us from the CURSE of the Law, having become
a curse for us."

We are no longer bound by the curse of the Law, having to keep the Law perfectly. Jesus made a way for us to be made right in God's eyes through *faith* in Jesus, who actually *did* fulfill the full requirements of righteousness under the Law. Now the demand of the Law, to obey it perfectly, no longer holds terror to us who are in Christ. We have a way to be forgiven if we stumble and break a law.

THE 10 COMMANDMENTS STAND APART

The 10 Commandments stand apart from the Old Covenant with its sacrifices and the New Covenant with salvation through faith in Christ. That's because the 10 Commandments are simply God's standard of righteous behavior until heaven and earth pass away. Jesus speaks clearly on this in Matthew 17:19;

> *"Do not think that I came to abolish the Law or the Prophets; I did not come to abolish but to fulfill.*
>
> *For truly I say to you, until heaven and earth pass away not the smallest letter or stroke shall pass away from the Law, until all is accomplished.*
>
> *Whoever then annuls one of the least of these commandments and so teaches others shall be called least in the Kingdom of Heaven.*
>
> *But whoever keeps and teaches them shall be called great in the Kingdom of Heaven."*

Jesus spoke these words with the full knowledge that He had come to abolish the sacrificial aspects of the Law; yet He upheld the 10 Commandments as part of the New Covenant! This is also confirmed by many scriptures throughout the New Testament, some of which are listed under the next heading.

THE LAW IS GOD'S STANDARD OF RIGHTEOUSNESS

The reason the 10 Commandments stand apart is this:

The Old Covenant was temporary for the forgiveness of sin, but it had no ability to change the heart. Forgiveness came through sacrificial offerings as mentioned. The imperfect covenant passed away when the time came for Jesus, the Perfect Sacrifice, to be offered. Now through Jesus and the Holy Spirit we are both forgiven and changed in our heart to desire obedience. The question is - obedience to what? Well, God has spelled out exactly what obedience is. His standard of righteousness is defined in the 10 Commandments and Jesus' explanation of them in the Sermon on the Mount. If the standard of righteousness is thrown out with the old covenant sacrifices, confusion results! We end up reverting back to the time with the Israelites when every man did what was right in his own eyes. Worse yet, obedience becomes following impulses, urgings and voices. These are very often misleading and sometimes even demonic. Sincere people wanting to obey God end up doing things contrary to the standard set up by God because they were following a prompting that led them to believe a certain  law of God did not apply to them in this or that circumstance. This is precisely the state that much of the church in western countries has fallen into.

THE COMMANDMENTS BECOME THE RULE OF LIFE

This is not to say that God does not lead His people or even speak to them. In many extreme circumstances God has marvelously led His people. However, as a rule of living for all men and women at all times He has given us the guidelines of what will please Him. So the super Christian and the ordinary believer functioning in the workplace have same exact rules of behavior for what is acceptable to God. Every impulse and every leading must be subjected to the written Word of God.

The 10 Commandments are not the means of our salvation, but they have become our rule of living. This is historic, orthodox Christianity. Now we obey them because we love God for what He has done for us in Jesus. We *want* to obey them! By this we know that we have truly been saved and touched by God - if we *want* to obey. This is abundantly testified in the Scriptures,

> *Matt. 5:19 "Whoever keeps and teaches them [the command-ments] shall be called great in the Kingdom of Heaven."*

> *Matt. 19:17 "there is only one who is good; but if you wish to en-ter into life keep the Commandments."*

> *John 14:21 "He who has My commandments and keeps them, he it is that loves Me; and he who loves Me shall be loved by My Father and I will love him."*

> *John, 15:10 "If you keep My commandments, you will abide in My love."*

Romans 3: 31 "Do we nullify the Law through faith? May it never be! On the contrary we establish the Law."

Ephesians 6:1-3 Paul teaches the commandments; "Children obey your parents in the Lord for this is right. Honor your father and mother [which is the first commandment with a promise], that it may be well with you and that you may live long on the earth."

Titus 2:14 "Who gave Himself for us that He might redeem us from every lawless deed and purify for himself a people for His own possession, zealous for good deeds."

1John 2:3 "By this we know that we have come to know Him, if we keep His commandments.

1John 3:24 "And the one who keeps His commandments abides in Him and He in him. And we know by this that He abides in us, by the Spirit whom He has given us."

1John 5:3 "For this is the love of God, that we keep His commandments and His commandments are not burdensome."

This last verse is one of the finest tests of our relationship with God. If we go to church and find ourselves either having no thought about God's laws or straining against them, we have probably not met Jesus yet, we're just going to church. If we find that we're always trying to justify the things we're doing and are always pushing the limits to what our church will allow, we are also still in darkness. If however, we come into a lively personal relationship with Jesus we will find we can say like David did, that the laws of God are *"Sweeter than honey and the drippings of the honeycomb."* When Jesus enters our life we desire to obey, we love to obey and His laws are not burdensome but beautiful to us.

When we are truly born again, our only real grief is that we're not following God more closely. We are grieved that we still find ourselves sinning and following His commandments so imperfectly. We want to obey not only the letter of the law but also the heart of the law. We pour over the Scriptures to find all that God wants of us. We use the law of God as a mirror to see if there is any offensive behavior in us. This is what James is referring to in James 1:25,

"But the one who looks intently at the perfect law, the law of liberty, and abides by it, not having become a forgetful hearer but an effectual doer, this man shall be blessed in what he does."

LESSON 7

THE DEVIL'S JOB

As we examine the Commandments we find there are eight things *not to do* and two things *to do*. Eight specific things God has commanded we *must not* do and two specific things we *must* do. These, along with their New Testament counterparts, are the most important things God desires to see in our lives. Because they are so important to God they are also important to His enemy.

The devil has a job on planet Earth and he does his job very well.  You could almost say he is a perfect devil. His design is to lead us into death by separating us from the source of life. Sin is what separates us from God, the source of life. Since God has defined exactly what sin is the devil just works off the same list! This perfect devil's job is to meet us first thing every morning and do everything in his power to make us *do* every Commandment that we're told *not* to do and *not do* every command we're supposed to *do*. He loves his work and that's why it's so easy to be bad and so hard to be good. The devil sets himself against us every day to cause us to do the very things that offend God. That is why even if we've had the privilege of growing up in a Christian home we can't be content to think that we're not subject to the gross temptations of the world or that we'll automatically be good. In fact quite the contrary! Every single one of us from the worst murderer to the most innocent little girl growing up in a Christian home is born with the exact same *sinful nature*. Those who are pure and striving after righteousness become the particular target of God's enemy. It's part of the cost of discipleship.

When our first parents, Adam and Eve, disobeyed God, corruption came into their lineage. God told them it would happen. That lineage is us and the corruption affects every part of us. It affects the way we think, the way we act, the way we talk and the way we react to one another. It is so complete that even when we're born we are filled with selfishness. The ruler of this world, the devil, takes full advantage of this fact and constantly works to incite ill will, fights, arguments and disagreements. The whole world comes under his influence and our natural inclination to do wrong works right along with him so that corruption fills the earth. When the devil walks to and fro throughout the earth and sees everything nice and filthy he is quite satisfied with himself! All he has touched is corrupted. But

if he happens to see something gleaming in the distance he's alarmed. If he finds it is something clean and white, such as a group of God's children who have received Christ and are putting to death the deeds of the flesh, he is outraged! He doesn't leave the ninety-nine to seek the one who is lost; he leaves the ninety-nine lost to seek the one who is saved! He doubles and triples his efforts to cause them to stumble. That's why we must be constantly on guard. 1Peter 5:8 says *"Be sober of spirit, be on the alert. Your adversary the devil prowls about like a roaring lion seeking someone to devour."* If this seems foreign to you make it a point to read the Christian classic 'Pilgrims Progress.'

OUR HUMAN NATURE WORKS WITH HIM

Since the devil works overtime to get us to break as many of the Commandments as possible, we often find ourselves mired in sin. Thank God we can go back to Jesus again and be washed clean through repentance. Unfortunately though, when the devil makes us dirty we often don't *want* to be cleaned up right away. We want to stay dirty and keep thinking wicked thoughts and doing wicked things. It's our old nature to love sin and the devil takes full advantage of that weakness. So, how do we get out of this situation?

We find that the devil can only do things because we *let* him. He can't make us bad unless we *allow* him to. So we are really to blame. We open a door to the devil when he comes knocking offering us tantalizing temptations. God has established that through His help we can shut that door, if we earnestly address the problem instead of glossing over it. We won't be good instantly as we desire because of our old sin nature, but God has ordained that we can practice being obedient until it becomes a new habit. As we develop new habits over time, the urge to sin in those areas will diminish. It is very similar to starting music lessons. At

38

first our fingers do not and will not go into the right positions. We get discouraged; we want to give up. But as we keep it up and keep practicing, it becomes easier and easier. At some point we will even forget that at one time it was so difficult! That's how it is with obedience. If we persist and practice obedience through continual repentance, prayer and trusting God, He helps us start to improve until eventually what was a weakness will become a strength! Hebrews 5:14 says "But solid food is for the mature, who because of practice have their senses trained to discern good and evil."

OBEDIENCE IS BETTER THAN REPENTANCE

Once we receive Christ, we become a child of God. As His child we will be forgiven for our ongoing mistakes, but we will still be punished when we sin. Many people when they become Christians use their freedom in Christ to be careless in regard to sin. They figure that they are forgiven and if they sin, God will forgive them again. After all didn't Jesus Himself say that we must forgive someone who sins against us 70 x 7 times a day? [Matt.18; 22] Will He not also be as merciful to us? Yes, He will. If you repent, He will forgive you as many times as you sin. However there is one small thing that is overlooked - you can be forgiven but the consequence of sin still remains. Many have heard of life changing conversions that take place on death row. A convicted murderer confesses his sins and becomes a child of God. He is forgiven, but he will still pay for his crime with a life sentence or with capital punishment. The consequence of his crime remains - the one he murdered is still dead even though the murderer is filled with the joy of forgiveness. Or take the case of a young woman who commits the sin of fornication. She sleeps with her boyfriend and becomes pregnant. In the anguish that follows she may turn her life over to Jesus, but she will still have that child the rest of her life or the guilt of abortion. The forgiveness is real but the consequences still follow.

DISOBEDIENCE ALWAYS BRINGS PUNISHMENT

Another reason that obedience is better than repentance is this: when we become a child of God, God becomes our Father! As a good and true parent He disciplines us strictly when we disobey Him! Proverbs

39

3:11&12 says;

"My son do not reject the discipline of the Lord, or loathe His reproof, for whom the Lord loves He reproves, even as a father the son in whom he delights."

A child of the world, unrepentant and stubborn, experiences the wrath of God. His punishment for sin is poured out on the 'sons of disobedience.' They reap the full consequences of their sinful actions. As a child of God we don't escape punishment for sinning just because we're forgiven, because God disciplines His people! The difference is that the nature of the punishment changes. In the case of unrepentant sinners the punishment is unto death. In the case of the children of God the punishment is unto life. God's love for us is most clearly demonstrated by His unfailing discipline toward us. He does not want us to be harmed by the dangers of sin. He mercifully and diligently corrects and chastises His beloved children. So in every case sin leads to punishment. If you are a sinner you are punished as the just penalty for breaking the law; if you are a Christian you are punished in order to lead you into a pure life.

We see this clearly in the life of King David. He is called a man after God's own heart, yet he sinned grossly on several occasions. On each occasion the punishment of God followed. When he called for a census of the people against God's wishes, God forgave him, but He also caused a plague to spread through Israel which wiped out a large portion of David's men. When he committed adultery, God forgave him, but as a punishment the child of Bathsheba was allowed to die. Also, because of the magnitude of the sin God caused David's wives to be publicly defiled. So it is a grievous mistake to think that we can

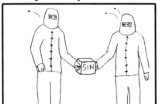

deal loosely with sin just because we can be forgiven. Ours is to deal with sin as though it were the most dangerous thing on earth. It is! We must be afraid of sin, we must learn to fear sin. We must study to learn what the laws of God are and then be afraid of breaking them. God warned Adam and Eve that on the day they sinned they would die. No, we will not drop dead immediately after we do something wrong, however, sin breeds sin and the further we go the harder it is to *want* to turn around. That separation will eventually lead to death unless we truly repent.

40

LESSON 8

THE THIRD COMMANDMENT

With the devil focusing on the 10 Commandments as the quickest, most effective way to separate people from God, he then proceeds to try to get the world to break each and every one of them. What better way to plunge people into complete disobedience than to get them to do the opposite of what God said without them even knowing it? So he gets them to fill their lives with false idols without any idea of what they're doing. They run from idol to idol from morning to night and never realize they are reaping the penalty of breaking the first commandments.

Next he turns his attention to the Third Commandment; *Thou shalt not take the name of the Lord thy God in vain.* By his skill and craft he is able to have the name of the Lord used as a curse word. It is not just *a* curse word, it is *the* curse word. It is the most common and acceptable form of cursing. So that when other words are banned from public media as distasteful, the sacred name of Jesus can be defamed from morning to night without any repercussion.  Can you imagine the outcry if the name Allah were used as a curse word on television? On that subject, have you ever wondered why we don't yell 'oh Buddha' or 'oh Hare Krishna' or 'Mohammed' when things go wrong? It's because Satan knows it doesn't matter how many times we use Buddha as a curse word, it doesn't have any effect on separating us from God. No, his design is to hurt us as much as possible, so he mysteriously puts the name of God and Jesus into the mouths of people when they're angry. He knows that if Jesus is used as a curse word it will separate us from God. Once he separates us from God, he will be able to shepherd us into hell with very little resistance.

DO NOT FOLLOW THE MULTITUDE IN DOING EVIL

Another of his tactics is to cause a law of God to be broken so frequently that it no longer is considered a law by most people. Take the example of posted speed limits on our various roads and highways. In New England, if not throughout the country, the speed limits are so routinely ignored that if someone was ticketed in a 65 mph zone for going only 75 mph the driver would be irate! Why? Because the traffic flows ordinarily at 80-85 mph. The posted limits have ceased to exist because it has become acceptable to greatly exceed them without any concern for breaking the law.

In the case of the Third Commandment we have a similar situation. This law has been so routinely ignored that it ceases to be a law in the minds of the people. They think it can be broken with impunity, that nothing will happen to them. If they were to be punished for taking the  Lord's name in vain they would be irate! They would complain that everybody does it and that they were being unfairly treated! However the Scriptures say "Do not follow the multitude in doing evil" [Exodus, 23:2]. There is no excuse that will stand up to God's all penetrating gaze. Ours is to study the requirements and abide by them no matter what the rest of the world is doing. When we die we will stand before God alone. The multitude we followed in doing evil will not be there to defend us. The full Third Commandment reads,

"You shall not take the name of the Lord your God in vain, for the
Lord will not leave him unpunished who takes his name in vain."
That means every single time we hear the Lord's name used as a curse word, punishment is being assigned - on TV, on videos, in the work place. He will not leave them unpunished even though everybody does it. The book of Leviticus 5:17 says,

"Now if a person sins and does any of the things which the Lord
has commanded not to be done, even though he was unaware,
still he is guilty and will bear his punishment."

GOD DOES NOT FORGET BECAUSE IT IS *HIS* NAME

Imagine for a moment that your own name was used as an exclamation every time something annoyed people. And imagine that it was not just generically your name - Nicholas or Jennifer - but

42

it was you specifically out of all those with your name that they were referring to! Next, try to imagine what it would be like to be able to hear your name being used as a curse in every workplace, every office, every factory, in every bar and restaurant and in every home! Jesus hears His name used that way 24 hours a day. What a hurtful way to treat the One who loves us to the end of time!

We spoke of the Commandments not being burdensome to us and they are not. If we imagine the tender heart of Jesus enduring that type of abuse, it makes us desire to speak His name lovingly and reverently. Picture what a wonderful soothing fragrance it is to our Dear Savior when He hears one of His beloved children speak His name tenderly in the midst of the great din of curses. He is our dearest friend, our truest love and our greatest joy. Our loving use of His name can actually be a comfort to Him and make all His pains for us seem worthwhile. God is a person, not a 'force.'

PICTURE THIS

Picture yourself as a student at a school. Say one hot day on the way home you decide to go for a swim at the lake. While you are a long way out suddenly your leg cramps up. You start to panic and then begin to go down. A school mate sees you in trouble. This particular school mate is someone a little different from everyone else and a little misunderstood. He also can't swim. But without a moment's hesitation he rushes in to try to save you. Somehow he manages to reach you and pull you to safety. You're safe and alive! As you look around in relief however, you find that your rescuer is nowhere in sight. In the midst of saving you he's taken on so much water that he's gone under. The sad conclusion is that he has drowned. You're in shock and disbelief at his utter selflessness. He not only risked his life but actually went to his death rescuing you. You're overwhelmed that such a person could even exist on earth.

After the funeral things return to normal. One day, as you're walking down the hall you hear someone mention his name. But something is wrong. It's not in a good way, but as a scornful joke! Did you hear correctly? Were they actually mocking the very person who gave his life for you? They're making fun of him because he was so stupid as to jump in the water when he couldn't swim. They mock him because he could save you but not himself! Then somehow it becomes a fad at school. Suddenly whenever something goes wrong everyone uses his name as a swear word! Imagine how you would feel. But that's just the beginning. Then it becomes so pervasive that you found *yourself* thinking it! Eventually his name slips out of your *own mouth* as a curse. Try to imagine the injustice of that. From this we can see how terribly wrong it is to use Jesus' name as a curse. Not only must we resist the tide of a society that mocks Him continually, but we should be indignant towards those who defame our Savior who gave His life to save us.

OTHER USES OF SWEARING
PROHIBITED BY THE COMMANDMENT

In the Biblical context we see there are other meanings for the word swear which are also prohibited by the Third Commandment.

a] One use means to swear *by God*. That is an oath or a vow using the name of the Lord to add emphasis. A case for this might be along the lines of 'I swear, by God, if that man ever steps on my property again I'll call the police and have him thrown off.' This is invoking God to be a witness that you will do the thing you say. The truth is you have no assurance that you will even be alive tomorrow. And God may determine that the next time He sees *you* He'll have *you* thrown out! This is a very common abuse of this commandment and we see it all the time. Another common usage would be to swear by God that by this time next year you will have accomplished this or that goal. This is particularly the meaning that Jesus was warning against in the Sermon on the Mount. He instructs us in Matthew 5:34-37 not to make *any* vow that we will do something. He teaches that men should be humble and realize they have no power to absolutely determine the outcome of events. Instead we are to simply say 'I hope to do this or that and if God enables me I will accomplish it.' [James 4:15] When man makes an oath before God he fails to recognize that the events of the earth are sovereignly determined by God alone. Proud man

is not able to absolutely determine the outcome of his intentions. That is God's domain. When man makes a firm vow to do something, no matter what, he is tempting God to thwart him. Remember the Titanic.

b] Another common case of using God's name in vain has to do with invoking His holy name as though it were a magic power. This is seen in the case of the seven sons of Sceva mentioned in Acts 19:13-16. They attempted to cast out a demon using the name of Jesus without proper knowledge or reverence. They were trying to use God's holy name as a powerful word to accomplish their purposes. The result was that God left them to their own devices. The demons fell upon the brothers and greatly harmed them.

This misuse of God's name is far more prevalent than you would guess. Whenever we use any of God's names as part of a 'formula' to accomplish a specific purpose, we are entering dangerous ground. God's name cannot be used that way. It is called *conjuring* and uses the name of God as magic. Whenever you are taught that this prayer works for this problem and that prayer works for that problem, you are in forbidden territory. Or if you are taught to pray exactly in a certain way, again you are using God's name as a magic formula. Sadly, this is now quite common in many modern churches. This does not include written prayers that are read as part of a liturgy, it refers to formulated prayers that will supposedly achieve a certain result. Jesus is a person not a force. The God of the Bible knows every intention of the thoughts of your heart. He cannot be forced or tricked into doing something for you because you prayed in a certain way. That is foolishness. We need no formulas with God. A simple heartfelt prayer is all it takes to get the attention of our loving Father who knows our needs before we ask.

c] Another example of taking God's name in vain is when teachers or evangelists teach false doctrine in the name of Jesus. The precious lambs are led astray and devoured by these 'prophets' who systematically rob and plunder the unsuspecting. All the while they use the name of Jesus to justify and qualify their deeds. God's wrath will not be slow to visit those who speak falsehood in His name, misleading the very ones He died to save.

d] Finally, there is using the Lord's name in vain before a magistrate. In most modern courts in the free countries when a person is called upon to testify he must take an oath before God to tell the truth, the whole truth and nothing but the truth. If a person commits perjury or lying under oath he is guilty of a crime before the law. Depending on who the person is he may or may not get in trouble with the law. However, there is another penalty that he will not be able to escape no matter how high priced his lawyer is. The law of God makes it clear that if we take an oath before a judge with God as our witness that we are telling the truth, we better be telling the truth. God will not hold him guiltless who uses His name in vain. The penalty will be assigned by God and sent to the one who lies under oath.

FASCINATING FACT:

Did you know that the phrase 'to tell truth, the whole truth and nothing but the truth' used in our modern courts was taken from Martin Luther's catechism, under the heading of keeping the Second Commandment? It was written approximately 250 years before the U.S. judicial system adopted it!

LESSON 9

THE CLASS ROOM

In the last lesson we covered a verse which needs to be reviewed again: Leviticus 5:17 which says,

"Now if a person sins and does any of the things which the Lord has commanded not to be done, though he was unaware, still he is guilty and shall bear his punishment."

When students enter a college class they are immediately handed a syllabus which contains all the vital information about the course. If the students miss an exam date or a deadline for a paper or project they will automatically receive a bad grade. If the students then go to the professor to complain that they didn't know, the professor will simply say, "It's in the syllabus, didn't you read it?" The teacher requires the students to be responsible enough to look over the course requirements. It is assumed. The failing grade is entered because it was the student's job to know the requirements.

In the same way, God has laid down all the class requirements for our time as a student on earth. Everything that is necessary to do well has been laid out clearly and logically. There are no surprises, no tests or quizzes on material that hasn't been covered. In fact it is an open book test! If we fail, it's simply because we didn't pick up the book. If we go to God and say 'I didn't know,' He will say, 'It was all written out for you, why didn't you read it?' Ignorance will not stand as a excuse. So breaking the law will result in penalty no matter what and keeping the law will result in reward no matter what. Ours is to quickly and thoroughly study the laws of God so we can stop breaking them and paying the penalty, start keeping them and receiving the  reward. The happiest people you have ever met are those who most closely obey God's laws. Those who follow the syllabus of God are those who have obtained true wisdom. Proverbs 8 says,

"For wisdom is better than jewels; and all desirable things cannot compare with her."

"The fear of the Lord is to hate evil."

"Those who diligently seek me shall find me. Riches and honor
are with me, enduring wealth and righteousness"
"Now therefore O sons, listen to me, for blessed are they who
keep my ways"
"Heed instruction and be wise, and do not neglect it"
To those who ignore God's instructions, He says,
"For he who finds me finds life and obtains favor from the Lord"
"But he who sins against me injures himself; all those who hate
me love death"

MEDIUMS AND SPIRITISTS

We're going to add a few interesting detours on our study of the
Commandments. So this next law is a little known and often neglected
rule which is found in Leviticus 20:6. It says,
"As for the person who turns to mediums and to spiritists to play
the harlot after them, I will also set my face against that person
and will cut them off from among his people."
It is not necessary to ask you to take a look in the back of any
women's magazine to see what you will find there, because it is a given
that there will be pages of advertisements for mediums, spiritists, astrologers and those with 'special insight.' Madame Z is quick to offer
supernatural advice to naive women seeking love and happiness, for a
price. If you interview those women who take her up on the offer you
will find a surprising thing. If you ask them if they believe in God, the
vast majority will say yes! Ask them if there is anything wrong with
consulting fortune tellers, mediums, tarot cards or astrologers, they
will say no. What does this show? The vast multitude of inquirers
have not read the syllabus! They do not know the course requirements.
Therefore, they will receive the penalty for failing to obey. Ignorance
is not an excuse. If they read the syllabus, they would know that it
is strictly prohibited to do those things and that a heavy penalty will
come to those who do. God's face will be against you. And why is it
so serious? Because it is again a breech of the First Commandment,
you shall have no other gods before Me. When people consult with
mediums and astrologers, they are many times actually consulting
demonic entities. Two penalties will ensue.

The first penalty for breaking God's law is the punishment that it separates us from Him and causes us to be empty and devoid of life. The second is built into the sin. The devil is called the 'father of lies' in the Bible. That is both his title and his job description! His underlings carry out his desire to deceive people to their own destruction. So the words received from those sources, are by nature, meant to confuse people and send them in the wrong direction. The devil's greatest glee is to lure people to some wonderfully desirable object, an object that *looks* like the fulfillment of all their dreams. What they don't know is that the object is actually the opposite of what they think it is. It's toxic and will destroy their lives.

A simple and oft used formula is as follows: a young woman from a Christian home follows the multitude in doing evil by going to a fortune teller. She assumes it's innocent fun which 'everyone knows is harmless.' The naive girl is then directed by 'enlightened words' to look for a certain boy that will be her true love. She then finds the 'perfect guy' who also happens to do drugs, drinks heavily and is abusive. But, because she feels she was supernaturally directed she believes she will be able to change him and everything will be all right. So she enters a self-destructive relationship and her life is thrown away. That is the nature of the enlightened words from mediums, astrologers, spiritists and their 'Christian' counterparts, the wolves in sheep's clothing, the false prophets.

MORE INTERESTING LAWS

According to Proverbs 6:23-27 this next command is a lamp, and its teaching is light.

"Keep from the evil woman, from the smooth tongue of the
   adulteress.
   Do not desire her beauty in your heart, nor let her catch you with
   her eyelids.

For on account of a harlot one is reduced to a loaf of bread.
An adulteress hunts for the precious life.
Can a man take fire in his chest and not be burned?
Or can a man walk on hot coals and his feet not be scorched?
So is the one who goes in to his neighbors wife."

Consider for a moment the truth of this law. It is a law which no one knows and yet it is law which never fails. If you do a little research into current events, you will see this law being proven over and over again. The pages of the latest newspapers and magazines declare the existence of God! His laws written down thousands of years ago direct the course of modern events. Let's take a look.

If you examine the leading men of the business world, you will find that almost without exception the most successful and wealthy over a long period of time are those who are good family men. They have been married to the same person for many years *and they haven't been unfaithful.* Of course there are always rich and glamorous people in the tabloids, but those usually vanish after their 15 minutes of fame. We're addressing corporate heads of large companies who have been building their wealth and reputation for a number of years. Look closely at their lives. As soon as they begin to feel confident and decide to take on a mistress, God's Word comes into effect. No matter how powerful or well-connected they are they will end up in deep disgrace. God's laws are unrelenting and irresistible. The next time you look, many of those same men will be dishonored and looking for a job, just as the scripture reads, "they are reduced to a loaf of bread." Do a study on your own and see if these things are not so. Proverbs 7:25 -27 says;

"*Do not stray into her paths, for many are her victims she has cast down and numerous are all her slain. Her house is the way to hell, descending to the chambers of death."* It is a fearful thing to break the laws of God. To be ignorant of them is like walking through a mine field with no map! How many other unstoppable rules are there that we ourselves might run through?

ILL GOTTEN GAINS DO NOT PROFIT

Proverbs 10:2 says, *"Ill gotten gains do not profit."* If you wanted to prove scientifically the existence of God, this one law is all you would need. If you were to carefully observe the transactions of man you would find this an unfailing example of God's providential ruling over the 'sons of men.' God is a God of supreme justice. He is present at all the dealings of men. As Thomas Aquinas explains, He watches every transaction and is intimately concerned for the justice on each side. He watches the balance to make sure it is equal. Let's consider how easy it is to have ill gotten gain.

It can mean outright stealing. Don't do it. There is no profit in stealing. Our house was burglarized once. A lot of electronics were stolen. We calculated the value of the goods, subtracted the fencing fees, deducted the cost of gas and tolls and found they could have made more money with one hour of honest labor than all the hours of breaking in and driving around, not to mention the fear of being caught! By the time we examined it closely we actually felt sorry for them! It is a pitiful waste to try to profit from ill gotten gain.

However, there are many ways to steal. Though most people in this study group would hardly consider the notion of burglarizing, almost every one engages in some form of stealing. If you consider unreported income as stealing tax money from the government you would find many people shifting uncomfortably in their chairs! How about selling some item such as a used car for more than it's worth? Say there is a mechanical problem that hasn't become noticeable yet and we want to get rid of the car while we can? God is intimately concerned with the justice of the transaction. He is, in this case, on the side of the buyer, against us! Thomas Aquinas addresses this brilliantly in his Summa Theologica. It is worth looking up. God is on both sides. Do not assume He's with you. What He wants to see is a fair transaction.

Or you might find a great bargain at an antiques show or a wonderful piece of workmanship by some unknown artisan. Because you know the person is desperate for money you haggle him down to far below the value of the item. You go home bragging about your purchase, but is God pleased with it? Isn't He much more likely on the side of the dealer or craftsman? He will make your treasure to become of no pleasure to you and he will exact the fair price from you!

In business there are thousands of ways to cheat, to undercut, to sell poor merchandise. We must be vigilantly on guard to make sure no ill gotten gain enters our hands. God will require it of us.

This is not a prophecy, but a prediction based on the irrevocable Word of God; those companies, especially credit companies that prey on the poor and unsuspecting by excessive interest rates, impossible terms and unrealistic late penalties will find themselves face to face with the true Judge. Every time they have caused the poor to cry out in anguish because of a credit bill that is impossible to pay off, they will find God will require it of them. God is on the side of the oppressed. The investment companies that boast of 20% and higher returns will be confronted by an angry God. They may have found loop-holes to conduct business on earth without being illegal, but there is a higher law. The law of God states that ill-gotten gain made on the backs of the oppressed will not profit them. On the contrary, it will be their undoing.

LESSON 10

THE FOURTH COMMANDMENT

"Remember the Sabbath Day to keep it holy.
Six days you shall labor and do all your work,
But the seventh day is a sabbath of the Lord your God;"

We hear much talk these days about the idea that Jesus saves, but very few people understand what He saves us from. For the most part we picture being saved from hell like being rescued from a burning building. That is true eventually, but that is the result of what He actually saves us from. As we read in Matthew 1:21, Jesus came to save us from our *sins*. To be forgiven is one thing. There is great relief in being forgiven especially if you have done something very wrong. However, the real work is to change us so that we don't do that wrong thing again! That is the heart of God's salvation. Psalm 103 says; *"He pardons all our iniquity and heals all our diseases."* Our real disease is sin.

THE RULES OF THE HOUSE

The aim of any good parent is not to simply forgive their children for doing wrong things, it is to make them good kids. The pattern for a good parent was taken from God. So as a good parent, God laid down the rules of the house - the Moral Law. He has written out the rules of proper behavior for living in His house. *We are not saved because we follow the rules but because we are saved, we want to follow the rules and must obey them.* Again, this is the almost forgotten historical Gospel. We are saved by His grace and lovingkindness; then He desires us to start being good kids! How do we know what is expected of us? Is it different for each person? We're often pressured to think we must hear a voice inside us telling us what to do. This is not so. God has made the rules of the house the same for everybody. *If we want to know what God's will is for us, all we have to do is post the 10 Commandments and the Sermon on the Mount on the refrigerator and we know what God's will is for us!* His will is for us to be good and obey the rules of the house. He indeed may have specific tasks for certain people, but all of us know what His daily will is.

53

As we know, it is very difficult to simply stop doing everything that is wrong and every soul-deadening distraction. Why? Because, for the most part, our lives are completely filled with those ungodly pastimes. To stop them is to leave a huge void in our lives. Those are the things we live for. But God has ordained that the bad is not simply removed from our lives but that it is replaced by something better. That makes it easier to let go of the old. Say you were being evicted from an old tumbled-down shack where you lived. It wasn't much, but it was your home and you were comfortable there in spite of it stinking and being piled high with junk. The Board of Health has come by and condemned the property and asked you to vacate. You are furious. What right do they have to come and tell you where you can or can't live? You threaten to call lawyers and city officials. There's no way you're going to leave.

In the middle of your ranting, a lady comes up to you from another agency and says that they have obtained a beautiful condominium for you to move into at no cost. Suddenly you stop. Suddenly, you can't wait to get your things and get moving. With the anticipation of the new you hardly even remember the old! Now, the transition is easy. That is how God deals with us. He never takes anything away that He doesn't replace with something a thousand times better. That's why it is such a pleasure to follow Him and obey Him. The heart of this Commandment is just that - God gives us a wonderful gift that makes following Him a delight.

IT IS A COMMANDMENT
OF MAJOR IMPORTANCE TO GOD

Many people assume that honoring the Sabbath is merely a nice suggestion for stores to be closed on Sunday. God, however, treats the Sabbath as a foundation stone in the lives of His true followers.

Honoring the Lord's Day is of major importance to God. The Sabbath was established at the beginning of time. Genesis 2:3 says,

> *"Then the Lord blessed the seventh day and sanctified it, because in it He rested from all His work which God had created and made."*

God also established that the Sabbath was eternal,

> *"It is a sign between Me and the sons of Israel forever, for in six days the Lord made heaven and earth, but on the seventh day He ceased from labor and was refreshed." Exodus 31:17.*

God reiterated the Sabbath when He ordained the various appointed times,

> *"For six days work may be done; but on the seventh day there is a Sabbath of complete rest.*
> *You shall not do any work; it is a Sabbath to the Lord in all your dwellings." Leviticus 23:3.*

God spoke again to Isaiah the prophet many hundreds of years later reconfirming His concern with obeying the Sabbath;

> *"For My salvation is about to come and My righteousness to be revealed.*
> *How blessed is the man who does this, and the son of man who takes hold of it;*
> *Who keeps from profaning the Sabbath, and keeps his hand from doing any evil." Isaiah 56:1-2.*

The observance of the Sabbath is also established after the new heavens and the new earth are made!

> *"For just as the new heavens and the new earth which I make will endure before Me declares the Lord,*
> *So your offspring and your name will endure. And it will be from new moon to new moon and sabbath to sabbath.*
> *All mankind will come to bow down before Me says the Lord." Isaiah 66:22-23.*

From this we can correctly gather that the Sabbath is of great significance to us and to God. It will be celebrated in some form throughout eternity. Ours is to study carefully that we may enter into the true spirit that the Sabbath was designed for.

THE CORRUPTION OF THE COMMANDMENT

As we mentioned, our enemy, the devil, makes it his business to completely corrupt the Commandments. In nine of the ten Commandments his chief tactic has always been to water them down to the point that they are completely ineffective. He doesn't destroy the law; he just makes all type of sinful behavior acceptable while still under the guidelines of the law. The religious leaders of Jesus' day are a good example of this. They would follow the letter of the law by not killing someone, all the while doing everything in their power to harm anyone in their way. They could maliciously abuse the object of their wrath as long as they stopped just short of murder. They could engage in every type of coarseness and lustful behavior as long as they stopped short of actually committing adultery, as defined specifically by the Law. Adding to their guilt, if anyone outside their ruling class were caught in adultery they would have them stoned to death, all the while congratulating themselves on their innocence.

Jesus addresses this specifically in the Sermon on the Mount. He instructs us that the Commandment, 'Thou shalt not murder,' means that we should do nothing to harm anyone. We should not even speak words that would hurt them, much less cause any bodily harm. Regarding adultery, He said that the law means we should not even look lustfully at someone because the sin is still in the heart. So by shrinking the law to mean only the specific words that are used, the devil with the willing help of men is able to render the Commandments useless. All types of behavior are permissible while still maintaining our innocence under the law.

We said that is the devil's tactic for nine of the laws - watering them down. For the last one he changed his approach.

THE DREADED SABBATH

Rather than water this one down, the devil's method for ruining the Fourth Commandment was to exaggerate it and make it *more* than it is. So that instead of it being the blessing that God intended, it became a whole series of strict observances that turned God's Holy Day into God's *dreaded* day. That's why Jesus fiercely condemned the religious leaders. They had made the Sabbath abhorrent to the people.

So down through the ages, and through many reincarnations, religious leaders have made the Sabbath to be unbearable. They imposed heavy restrictions on the people, including things like making the children sit perfectly still and quiet for hours and hours. Dry readings and lengthy dull lectures added to the weight of the day. The world's reaction was predictable. As soon as the church weakened sufficiently to be unable to punish offenders, the world cast off the fetters of strict Sabbath observance and never looked back.

THE DAY FOR WORLDLY INDULGENCE

Though the remnants of overly strict Sabbath observance lasted right up till the middle of the 20th century, now it is impossible to imagine! Sunday has not only become a shopping day, but it has become *the* shopping day. There is not a flea market or craft show that doesn't promote Sunday morning as the premier shopping time. Sunday has become *the* day to drink beer and watch sports. Sunday has become *the* day to wash the pickup. Sunday has become *the* day for yardwork and every other chore that's been put off. Sunday has become *the* day for every car rally and race. Sunday is

the day for every type of worldly indulgence and sinful pastime. Ironically, most people pick their favorite Sunday diversion and observe it *religiously!*

Nor do the members of God's own family fare much better. After the obligatory services are over, Sunday now becomes the day to engage in every worldly pleasure. They have done their duty to God and now they are ready to have some fun. Sunday morning church is followed by Sunday afternoon abandon. Following church dismissal, it is impossible in many cases to recognize a Christian from a non-Christian. All the while, God's people content themselves that because they are not at their job per se they are fulfilling God's law! That sounds awfully familiar, doesn't it? So in all cases the Commandment is rendered useless, either by making it loathsome to the people or by making it a day of complete indulgence. God's enemy howls with laughter both ways. In one case, it is a heavy burden and a drudge, in the other, it is a day to indulge the fleshly desires.

FAMILY TIME

Imagine a parent working hard to support the family, coming home from work exhausted only to spend the rest of the evening cooking and caring for the children. The reward a parent gets for their labors is enjoying the times of sweet intimacy with their children. It is the only thing that makes all their work worthwhile. Now imagine [and this is not hard] that as the parent asks the children to spend the afternoon or evening with them, they are greeted by a chorus of whines and complaints. The kids would much rather be watching TV, or playing video games, or out with their friends. There is nothing more painful for a parent than this common scenario. At this point, the parent has the authority to insist on their presence, but what is the good of it? To have them physically present while their minds are distracted with other things is simply a heartbreak for the loving parent. So they abandon the attempt at family time. The kids are jubilant, but something has died in the father and mother. The reward for all their care has been taken from them and all that remains is the sheer drudgery of cooking, cleaning and paying bills.

THE TRUE FATHER

We have a true parent and a true Father who has done much more for us than cooking and cleaning. He has gone so far as to literally give His own Son for us. The Bible says we cannot even count the number of times His thoughts turn toward us in the day! He has engraved our names on the palm of His hand! God's reward for all His labor for us is no different from the ordinary parent's. His joy comes simply from having intimate time with His family. It is His delight and makes all His work worthwhile. Unfortunately, He often encounters the resistance common to earthly parents - He finds His children reluctant to come to Him. They would rather be watching TV or playing video games or out with their friends. They are too busy; chores around the house simply have the priority.

In the case of the overly strict Sabbath, it is the same as the parent *forcing* the children to have 'quality time' with them. It can be done but what is the use? God's heart is not warmed as the pews are, filled with bodies wishing they were someplace else. As the Sabbath is abandoned and everyone turns to his own pleasure, it is the same as the parent who simply gives up the idea of sweet family time entirely. It comes with a huge price. The parent becomes just a slave to the children and all joy in them is lost. Similarly with God, He still maintains His care. He still causes the sun to rise on the just and the unjust, but He takes no pleasure in it. The reward for His labors has been taken away. Keep in mind the often forgotten fact that God is a *person.* He is not a force. He is not far off and unaware of His people, but knows each one by name. He is intimately acquainted with us. It is not a matter of breaking a law by ignoring the Lord's Day; it is a matter of breaking a Great Heart.

GOD'S HEART

TRUE WORSHIP ON THE LORD'S DAY

The clearest picture of the Sabbath observance that will remain for eternity is found in Isaiah 58:13, 14.

"If because of the Sabbath you turn your foot from doing your
own pleasure on My holy day.
And call the Sabbath a delight, the holy day of the Lord,
honorable, and shall honor it, desisting from your own ways,
from seeking your own pleasure, and speaking idly,
Then you will take delight in the Lord, and I will make you ride
on the heights of the earth"

This passage addresses the issue of enjoying the company of the Lord. Even more, it speaks of delighting in Him. Now we can see the significance of it. Just as parents would be overjoyed to find the children glad to spend time with them, so would God! When His beloved come to Him willingly and with gladness, it warms His heart. It makes His labors for the world worthwhile. It is noteworthy that we, you and I, can cause delight to our Father! We can gladden Him and brighten His day!

There are those who claim God has no needs, and in a strictly theological sense, maybe they are correct, but it leaves out the most important element of God's fatherhood, that He has real feelings because He is a real person. Why would God be angry with the Israelites when they complained in the wilderness? Because He was delighting in bringing them to a wonderful place which they refused to enter. It was a blow to His father's heart. See how He speaks of these things in Ezekiel;

"how I have been hurt by their adulterous hearts which turned away from Me." Ezek. 6:9b

If He did not love them exceedingly He would not have cared if they lived in slavery or in abundance. We are made in His image. The things we see and feel are but small reflections of what springs from God. When we love God and spend time with Him, He apreciates our love. It is a feeling only a parent can have and comes from nothing that the child has done or not done.

At the end of the day, when all the mistakes have been made, all the disturbances quieted, all the wrongs forgotten, and the little one simply runs to mother and father and jumps into their lap, that is the moment every parent lives for. Nothing from the day is remembered, all is lost in the delight of each other's company. It is a brand new beginning and the reconciliation of all wrongs. We parents didn't design things this way. This is a blueprint and a pattern that has been copied from God Himself. He designed family love and made it to be the very core of the universe. The heart of the Sabbath is no more and no less than intimate family time with our Father and Brother Jesus.

This is a good place to reiterate that Christianity is a religion of grace. Going through the commandments is not to put us in fear and panic that God is counting how many infractions we've made in a day. No, we have been redeemed from the curse of the Law. It's simply meant to bring us to the place of Godly humility that we might see how much we need His grace. That is the big issue. When we see how often we break the least of the commandments it drives us to God with true heartfelt repentance. In that state of repentance we have become fragrant to God! Even if we are still stumbling, we are still clothed in Jesus' righteous robes and pleasing to God. It is humility and a spirit of repentance that is necessary to be right before Him. So don't panic, just be aware of how much we need His grace and then maintain a heart attitude of repentance. Humility is true personal revival not doing everything perfectly. Praise God for that!

LESSON 11

CALL THE SABBATH A DELIGHT

GOING TO CHURCH

Now that we understand that the purpose of the Sabbath is to delight in God's company and to give Him delight by giving Him our wholehearted attention, how do we actually carry it out? What does honoring the Lord's Day consist of? Jesus summed up the Commandments by saying we should:

> *"Love the Lord with all your heart, all your soul, all your mind and all your strength."* Mark 12:30.

If we keep those words in mind we will automatically honor the Lord's Day in accordance with its true purpose.

In our attendance at our local worship service, it means joining in with all our attention. It means subduing our thoughts which are frequently flying about into worldly distractions. Initially, it's hard work to turn our thoughts toward the study of God's Word. It isn't  our natural inclination, as you know. If our thoughts are unbridled we certainly don't give God pleasure in our company and that's the goal. We must consider the preaching of the Word to be food for our souls and develope a hearty appetite for it. When our minds are engaged actively in scriptural study, it's impossible not to be excited about our time with God.

But because there are all types of preachers, some who study diligently and feed their flock nutritious food and others who feel their job is to simply occupy the podium for the hours of 10:30 to 12:00 on Sunday, it is wise to consider where you attend church. If after diligent effort to pay attention you find it is impossible to become interested, you might inquire into another place of worship. *"For the ear tests words* [for true wisdom], *as the palate tastes food," Job 34:3.* If you are earnestly seeking God, your spirit will simply be left dry by someone not preaching the pure Word of God. Do not consider it your obligation to stay there even if people are 'nice.' Your eternal life is more important than formalities. If you take the lead in finding a Godly, diligent preacher, you will do more good for everyone than by staying put. The rule is to remember you're going there to be in God's presence and to delight in hearing His Word taught. That is the purpose of attending a church service.

YOUR OWN PLEASURE

In regard to the rest of the day it is wise to read Isaiah 58 every Sunday. That is the best guide for keeping your behavior pleasing to Him. It instructs us not to seek our own pleasure.
"If because of the Sabbath you turn your foot from doing your own pleasure on My holy day..."
That means forsaking the normal things which fill our day to be with God. Remember, as the divine Parent, God's heart will be grieved if, when He desires to see us, we would rather be out golfing or water-skiing. Every type of worldly entertainment fills our thoughts from morning to night. Surely we can leave those pursuits for a few hours to seek the One who created all for our enjoyment!

SPEAKING IDLE WORDS

Scripture says that we should desist from idle talk;
"And shall honor it, desisting from your own ways, from seeking your own pleasure and from speaking idly."
If there is one thing that keeps us from being pleasing to God it's the things we talk about. For the most part our conversation is on a very low level. How could it not be? Our input all week is from the world! If you consider the content of popular TV programming, that alone accounts for the lack of intelligence in most conversation. Since the media supplies nearly 100% of the topics, it necessarily means our general level of speech has to be low. By low, I mean coarse, vulgar, silly, senseless, degraded, offensive or about meaningless things. If you stop to listen, you will find hardly any speech that doesn't fall into those categories. We are subjected to it night and day, every day of the week, either by active choice or simply because we exist here and can't get away from it. It colors all our thoughts and all our words. Most conversation seems to focus on the latest media stars and their recent hits, what they're doing and who they are with. It escapes our notice that in a few short years the most attractive of them will be wrinkled

and haggard. A few years after that and they will be in the eternal dungeons and all those who followed them will be there with them. Our heroes of the arenas will be retired with leg injuries and bad backs. They will have no more sympathy than remembrance. Like a horse with a broken leg they will have no more use to their owners or fans. They will die forgotten and those who followed will be even more obscure.

But *"The righteous will be remembered forever."* *[Psalm 112: 6]* It is surely to our greatest advantage to forsake these idols for a few moments to seek the Lord of the living. *"Behold I am coming quickly and My reward is with Me."* *[Rev. 22: 12]* For those who honor the Sabbath and take delight in the Lord He will cause them to *"ride on the heights of the earth and feed on the heritage of Jacob."* *[Isaiah 58: 14]*

TAKE DELIGHT IN THE LORD

The greatest pleasure a human can experience is closeness with God. That is not a rhetorical statement. Closeness with God is not mere religious duties faithfully carried out. It does not consist in sitting in church more often. God is a person. When we spend real time with Him, He fills us with an indescribable peace and contentment. Down through the ages it has not been theology that set men's hearts aflame. It was the true presence of God that filled their soul with wonder and joy. Once a person has tasted the sweetness of God's presence they are never the same. They are able to endure the most painful tortures and persecutions for the unspeakable delight of closeness to Him. It is a peace that is not of this world and cannot be taken away. Psalm 36:7-9 speaks wonderfully of this.

"How precious is Thy lovingkindness O God! And the children of
men take refuge in the shadow of Thy wings.
They drink their fill of the abundance of Thy house; And Thou
dost give them to drink of the river of Thy delights.
For with Thee is the fountain of life and in Thy light we see light."
When King David wrote these words he was conveying a true experi-

ence he had with God. God was no mere formality to him. God was a reality, a fountain of joy, which enabled him to endure long years of unjust persecution. Entering this "secret place of the Most High," as he called it was his greatest pleasure and so remains the greatest pleasure to all who seek Him. If you have never experienced it, the idea of a completely transformed life is still a mystery to you. So now we'll go over some helps that will assist you in drinking freely from the fountain of life and entering in.

ENTERING THE PRESENCE OF GOD

Of all spiritual concepts entering God's holy presence is the most important. Why is that? Because once you meet Him personally He will lead you into all truth. If all books were destroyed, as has been attempted several times through history, if you were deprived of all fellowship, as many have been, and you were never able to be instructed again, if in spite of this you develop the habit of coming into God's presence regularly, you will victoriously survive. Why? Because God is a person. By spending intimate time with Him, He will keep you close to Him. *"Draw close to Him and He will draw close to you."* *[James 4:8]* We should never forsake His written word but if it were ever taken from us, God would uphold us, convicting us of sin and granting us peace if we are faithful to come to Him in prayer.

IT TAKES TIME AND ENERGY

Of all the elements that draw us close to God the most necessary ingredient is time. We can engage in all the ordinary means of seeking the Lord - we can pray, we can attend church meetings, we can read the Bible and we can listen to instruction, but all these things will not have the desired effect without the element of time. And what do I mean by time here? Just this; we must spend enough time in our seeking to actually find God.

He has ordained that those who seek Him must seek Him earnestly. Just as gold is not found lying on the ground to be seen by all who stumble over it, so the treasures of God are not strewn about for all to fall into. The more precious the metal the more diligent man must be to find it. Gold is earnestly sought out. It is mined with great

64

energy. During the gold rush years no hardship could slow down the industrious miners. They sought it through endless years of exhausting labor. At all times the goal of striking a rich vein was before them and it encouraged them to persist. In the same way, the riches of God's presence are there for the diligent. The one who is easily distracted will not enter in. It requires earnest effort and a determination to not lose sight of the goal.

GOD CANNOT BE HAD BY THE EASILY DISTRACTED

A common situation which arises is this: You decide to spend some time reading the Bible on Sunday afternoon in order to grow close to God. After 5 minutes, you remember something important that needs to be done. You try to keep on reading but your thoughts keep going back to what needs to be done. After 10 minutes, you get up and do whatever it is. An hour later, you're thinking you spent time reading but you don't feel any closer to God! God will not be had by the casual seeker. He will be found only by those who seek Him with all their heart. Deuteronomy 4:29 says:

"You will seek the Lord your God, and you will find Him if you search for Him with all your heart and all your soul."

Two different elements are involved in seeking Him earnestly. One is that God doesn't want to bestow His treasures on those who are not truly interested. They are too precious to be handled by the worldly-minded. He Himself warns not to cast His pearls before those who are ungrateful and unthinking. Rather He instructs us to seek Him as a treasure buried in a field. *"The kingdom of heaven is like a treasure hidden in the field, which a man found and hid; and from joy over it he goes and sells all he has and buys that field." [Matt. 13: 44].* We are to sell all we own in order to buy the field and thus obtain the treasure. That 'selling all' includes  gladly giving up all our worldly Sunday pursuits to seek Him. It means there is nothing more important to us than finding Him. It means forsaking the pleasure and company of the world for the pleasure and company of God. He will not be found easily, but He will be found by the earnest. Those who determine that they are not going to stop praying, reading the Word, and seeking the face of Jesus till they find Him will be rewarded.

He will come to that person tenderly and gently. He will begin to fill their heart and soul with an unearthly peace. They will look up and behold His face. Though He rarely shows Himself visibly it makes no difference. When our Dear Savior is present in the room with us we do not need to see with our physical eyes - we know He's there. His Divine Presence has been the comfort of untold Believers in the privacy of their homes, in the midst of their hectic workplace, in the face of shattering loss and in the confines of prison. He rewards those who seek Him.

YOUR ADVERSARY

The second reason you must be so determined in your approach to God is that you have an enemy who will stop at nothing to keep you from spending time with Jesus. That enemy doesn't sit by passively hoping that you won't start to pray, but he actively interferes whenever you decide to set your mind on the things above. You can count on the most amazing distractions popping up! If you have a dog or cat they will suddenly start demanding your attention or behaving in the most annoying way, the phone will ring incessantly, friends will come over, your stomach will start to growl, your head will be filled with wild thoughts. You will find it almost impossible to focus on God. This is a good sign! You are now approach-ing a danger area for the devil. He is afraid you will make real contact with the Living God. C.S. Lewis addresses this brilliantly in The Screwtape letters. When you begin to feel like the devil is screaming in your face, *press on*. Don't be intimidated, don't give up. You have the victory in Christ!

There is an interesting story in the Old Testament [2 Kings 13] which describes a Prophet of God coming to the king of Israel. He instructs the king to strike the ground with an arrow, but doesn't explain why. The king halfheartedly hits the ground three times then stops. The Prophet then rebukes him for being short sighted and says that God had intended to deliver him from all his enemies. The number of times he struck the ground would signify the number of times he would defeat the armies around him. His lack of diligence caused him to make only a small setback to his enemies. In the same way God desires to give us victory over our enemy. If we are halfhearted and lazy we will not accomplish all that God intends for us. If, however, we press on when confronted by all types of intimidating opposition we will gain a great advantage over our enemy.

WORLD WON'T MAKE TIME FOR YOU TO BE WITH GOD

If you are tempted to think that if you give in to the distraction you'll get right back to God, you are mistaken. This is a common scenario. You are set on praying and reading the Word and immediately an interruption occurs. Your thought is that if you simply take care of it, then you'll be free to seek God in peace. So you get up and spend an hour dealing with the situation, figuring that now you'll be uninterrupted in your devotions. If you forget all else remember this - *the world will never make time for you to be with God*. You will have to force the time from the world's greedy grasp. It will not surrender it easily or without a fight. If you plan to be with God, decide ahead of time that you want it more than anything else. If you don't you will never, ever, be able to 'find the time.' It won't ever be convenient to seek the Lord.

LONG DISTANCE

One of the most helpful methods of truly contacting God is to think of it as a long distance connection. Consider a case of calling a friend who is overseas. You could pick up the phone and dial the number, fully expecting him to be there, since you know you have the right number. You then begin to rapidly speak all that is on your mind. After a minute you hang up. You're happy and satisfied that you just contacted your friend. The only problem is that it takes two minutes to make the connection! Your friend hasn't even picked up the phone yet! So it is with many of our prayers to God. He is waiting to bless us with His company, with His fellowship, and we break contact before we've even gotten in touch with Him. Our prayers are cursory and ineffective

because they are spoken before we've even had an opportunity to really connect with God. Obviously, we know that this is not true in a literal sense since God is closer than our breath, but it is very much true in a practical sense. Our thoughts are clouded with exposure to the world. Our mind is darkened by all type of ungodly influence. It takes some time to empty ourselves of those distractions in order to establish real communion with God. We must work hard to focus all our thoughts on Him. This, if for no other reason, is what I mean when I say it takes time. The difference that a couple persistent minutes can make in our prayer life is infinite! Those who have tasted the delights of heaven are those who have taken whatever time is necessary to come into the Lord's presence.

WHY DO WE CELEBRATE THE SABBATH ON SUNDAY?

Traditionally, the Sabbath was observed on our modern Saturday. It was the custom of the Jews throughout history and continues to this day. So why do we Christians now celebrate the Lord's Day on Sunday? Good question!

There are very good reasons for it. The first is to make a very important distinction. As we mentioned previously, the Ceremonial Law was replaced by the coming of Jesus but the Moral Law remains. The Fourth Commandment is the only one which reflects *both the Ceremonial and Moral Laws*. To distinguish the aspect of observing the Sabbath for sacrifices from the aspect of resting and delighting in God, the Church Fathers began to honor the day following the Sabbath. In this manner the heart of the Sabbath as described by Isaiah is observed without confusing it with the parts of the Sabbath which are no longer relevant. Remember that the Sabbath and its improper observance was a big issue at the time of Jesus. His greatest anger was directed towards those who enforced a legalistic rigidity on that day. Those Jewish leaders were still very much around in the early church days. They were trying to impose the same legalism on the church.

Changing the observance of the Lord's Day to the next day brilliantly eliminated honoring the Sabbath as the Pharisees did, while establishing the true worship of God at least once a week.

The second reason for changing the day is that the Apostles gathered on the first day of the week [our Sunday] to worship and break bread together. It was the day that our Lord Jesus rose from the dead and so it seemed fitting to them.

It was with great integrity that the church kept the heart of observing the Sabbath by 'honoring the Lord's Day' while changing the day. If we keep that in mind, we will not fall into legalistic formalities and yet will give God special attention at least once a week.

There is a strong movement today to turn the Lord's Day back to Saturday and with it a near militant criticism of those who worship on Sunday. To that I say, God has given liberty to us to worship on the day of our conviction. It is a heart for spending time with God that is at the center of the commandment, not the day itself. As an aside, if you happen to find yourself criticized, you can state the items above then casually mention that you are in the same camp as Peter and the rest of the apostles who worshipped on Sunday!

DID PAUL SPEAK AGAINST THE SABBATH?

Paul the Apostle mentions these things in Romans 14:5,

"One man regards one day above another [referring to the Sabbath]*, another regards every day alike. Let every man be fully convinced in his own mind."* These words, if read without understanding, cause many to miss the point of what Paul was saying. They conclude that it's up to their own decision whether they want to obey the Fourth Commandment or not and consequently many abandon regular worship. That's not what was going through Paul's mind when he wrote these words. If we remember that the heart of honoring the Sabbath is delighting in God and spending time with Him, these words make perfect sense. To those saints who continually seek the Lord's face [as Paul did] all days *are* the same, *because they make all days the Sabbath!* Those who seek the Lord have a continual feast! So if in fact we diligently and earnestly pursue fellowship with Jesus on a daily basis honoring one day above another is for practical purposes irrelevant. We then honor all days as consecrated unto God.

LESSON 12

THE FIFTH COMMANDMENT

"Honor your father and mother, as the Lord your God commanded you, that your days may be prolonged, and that it may go well with you"

Proverbs 19:16 says, *"He who keeps the commandment keeps his soul, but he who is careless of his way will die."* This is particularly relevant in regard to keeping the Fifth Commandment because we find the penalty of death is connected to breaking this law in Leviticus 20:9. It says, *"If anyone curses father or mother let them be put to death."* These are strong words for a society in which cursing parents is so commonplace that it no longer even elicits a response from adults!

Say you are on the battlefield and the commander has just given the order to move out and attack the enemy. Because of setting up a defensive position you have to make your way out through a mine field first. The commander has given a detailed map of where the mines are buried along with the only safe route in and out. As you look out over

the field everything *looks* safe. All looks perfectly normal with rocks, grassy patches, insects and even birds landing here and there. It seems safe to your senses, but it is *not safe*. Just a few inches below the soil are deadly explosives that will rip you apart.

As long as you closely follow the map you are safe. If you become overconfident and start trusting your own excellent sense of direction and common sense, you will be destroyed!

So it is for those who *"follow a multitude in doing evil."* Just because the world around you speaks evil of adults does not make it *safe* to do so. Those land mines are all around you and if you get confident of your senses and decide to forge ahead in the direction you think is okay, you will surely die. The only way to get safely out of this world and into the next is to closely follow the map.

We spoke earlier of laws being broken so frequently that they no longer exist in the minds of the people and this is a prime example. Somehow it has now become acceptable for children of all ages to speak rudely and disrespectfully to adults including [or especially] parents and teachers. *And they appear to get away with it* and that is the illusion of the battlefield as you look out at the seemingly normal landscape. Those mines are still there. However the fashion may be to speak scornfully to authority, it is not in fashion with God. The penalty of the law will be sent out, addressed personally to each one who mocks his parents. That penalty will be forwarded from address to address until it catches up with the offender. There is no where to hide.

FRIGHTENING SCRIPTURES

Adding to the weight of the Fifth Commandment we have many other laws instituted by God regarding proper respect for parental authority. Consider just these two;

"He who curses his father or mother, his lamp will go out in time of darkness." Proverbs 20:20

This means there is a built in penalty attached to cursing your parents that includes being abandoned in the time of your need. God will also cause a blindness to the truth to settle into the mind of the one who is disrespectful so that he will not find Him. Perhaps one of the most frightening scriptures in the Bible deals with this particular area:

"The eye that mocks a father and scorns a mother,
the ravens of the valley will pick it out and the young
eagles will eat it." Proverbs 30:17

What makes the verse so frightening is the realization that God's word never goes forth without accomplishing its purpose. When we see how easy it is to break this commandment it is terrifying! How simple it is to be scornful to a parent who does something against our liking! It's as natural as breathing and if unchecked will cause us grave consequences. The purpose of this is not that we would be condemned but that we would simply realize how often we break this commanment that we might run to God with a repentant heart. The miracle of the New Covenant is that we can be forgiven rather than dying under the breech of the law. The realization of our sinfulness and the subsequent running to God for forgiveness constitutes the washing of our robes found in Rev. 22:14. *"Blessed are those who wash their robes that they might have the right to the Tree of Life."* After we come to Christ for salvation God expects us to use His grace and our faith to start becoming good children.

With that in mind, go into any classroom and observe the language and attitude which is used to address the teacher! When this scripture is fulfilled, the birds of prey will be satiated. Adding to this [or perhaps initiating it] are the modern movies which are made for youth. In many programs the parents are made to look like bumbling fools while the hero [a child] bad mouths them. Wisecracks and scornful comments are made to look cool and impressive. And so it has entered our society like a flood and there is no longer any conscience in the matter. Nor is this restricted to secular households! Some of the most tolerant of this type of disrespect are the good Christian parents! They do not realize that this form of 'love' will most certainly lead their precious ones into the fiery pit.

THE GREAT NET

If we think about it in an ordinary sense, why would children rise up against their parents, mocking them, scorning, talking back and disobeying them? This is very unnatural. Why would we hate the very people who feed us, clothe us, give us a protected place to sleep and love us? Parents do all these things and more for their children and you'd expect the children to love and appreciate them for it, but they don't. Why? Because they have an enemy who hates them. He knows that if he can cause a child to be disrespectful to his parents he can very likely collect his soul at the end of his life. He focuses on this area because it is so easy. If he can just get people to scorn their

parents he can separate them from God. He loves to destroy families and cause heart misery to parents but his real goal is separating them from God. As we look at society today it is no accident or coincidence that it has become normal and acceptable for children to talk back to their parents, teachers and all adults. They have an enemy that prowls about like a roaring lion and he devours those who step out of God's protection by willfully disobeying Him. So the children think they are cool and hip and better than their parents, but in reality their souls are being fattened up for a great feast in hell.

This is why we must learn to be afraid of sin. We must fear it. To mock or scorn parents is an unthinkable crime in God's eyes. That means not only the scornful words but the attitude behind them. That means every time we exhale loudly or roll our eyes or even harbor thoughts against our parents we will have a penalty stamped and sent to us. A bad one. Just by living in our modern world we will automatically break some very serious rules. We must all learn what the laws of God are, then we must be afraid of breaking them. Just like with Adam and Eve, the day we sin is the day we die. No, we don't drop dead when we talk back to our parents, but we separate ourselves from God who is the source of all life. That is true death.

PARENTS TAKE THE PLACE OF GOD

God in His divine providence has allowed men and women to share in His duties and joys. While He could easily have designed a way for infants to survive on their own, He entrusted them to parents who would then be able to partake in a small portion of His own fatherly nature. It is one of those mysteries that are too wonderful to fathom. He made men and women to share in the tenderness of caring for the helpless, watching with joy as they grow and learn. As a father, I can truthfully say raising children is the greatest joy in life.

Just as there are the physical needs that we tend to with all diligence there are, of course, spiritual needs. God often gives us more responsibility than we are comfortable with. In this case parents have the responsibility of raising children up with a love and reverence for God. *However*

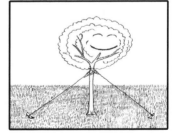

they raise them, that is how they are. We have the responsibility of raising them as citizens of heaven. If we don't, except for the direct intervention of God, they won't be.

A great part of that is teaching them proper respect for authority. We have a charge before God to prepare them to submit willingly and gladly to His own authority. They are like seedlings which are exposed to every type of buffeting. Contrary winds howl and storms blast upon them. We are their supporting wires that hold them straight until their trunks grow strong and their limbs firm. Once that young tree reaches a certain size no amount of pressure can bend it. As parents, that is our job. We are not our children's peers or playmates; we are their authority and guide. We have a task which we are accountable for that requires us to enforce heaven's laws even if it makes us unpopular for a short while.

It is my experience that in every case where the parents hold their ground to maintain discipline despite the threat of being 'alienated' from their children, they find in the end that the children return to them with wonderful affection. In all cases where the parents are afraid to stand their ground and give in to the children's pressure, the children end up disrespecting and despising their parents. Think about it.

THE FIRST COMMANDMENT WITH A PROMISE

On the wonderful side we have God's great blessing connected with honoring our parents! The commandment isn't that we should not think badly of our parents but that we should think well of them! As we do we will see a remarkable transformation of our 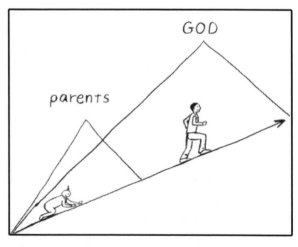 relationship with them. And as an added benefit it will also reduce our humiliation. It seems to be one of God's delights to show us our parents were right after we scoff at them!

74

LESSON 13

THE SIXTH COMMANDMENT

"THOU SHALT NOT MURDER"

In the previous lessons we have covered the fact that the enemy of our souls wants to get us to break as many commandments as possible. That is his master list. So he is always behind the scenes making it easy to break God's laws. If he can get us to break those laws, it will separate us from God. He works like a shepherd, gently herding the unwitting into hell. Since most people today don't even know the commandments let alone worry about breaking them, his job is easy. Society is filled up with the opposite of God's laws in media and conversation and it isn't even aware of the mortal danger it's in! That means for anyone who is interested in pleasing God they must be determined and diligent to seek out and learn His laws. By faith they will begin living a life which is completely contrary to the world around them. That's what personal revival is all about. We're here to provide support and friendship for those who wish to forsake all to follow Christ.

KILLING VS. MURDERING

We will now look at the Sixth Commandment: "Thou Shalt Not Murder." The first thing we must do is distinguish between killing and murdering. Killing is not prohibited by scripture, but murder is. The Bible allows killing under certain conditions. The Old Testament prescribes the death penalty for a number of crimes so that it is clear, according to scripture, the death penalty is justified for some crimes. The New Testament contains John the Baptist's admonition to soldiers to conduct themselves lawfully and not to complain. He does in no way tell them that they must leave the army. Here is evidence that the use of force is necessary to preserve order and is not a breech of the Sixth Commandment.

This is important because some Christian groups through the ages have misinterpreted this commandment to mean that we must never kill anyone for any reason. These become religious pacifists who refuse to fight for a just cause and speak loudly against the death penalty. Following that logic to it's conclusion, there would have been no one to stand up and fight against Adolf Hitler and he would have continued murdering Jews till there was none left! But God used the Allies as His 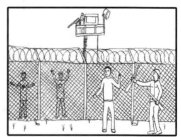 instrument to stop a maniacal dictator. Killing is justifiable under two conditions; first, in the event of war [King David was instructed by God to go to war] and second as a just punishment for serious crime after a fair trial [God instituted judges *and* the death penalty]. If intentional killing takes place outside of those conditions, it is no longer killing but murder.

TWO DEGREES OF MURDER

The Bible goes on to define different levels of murder. In Exodus 21:12-14 we find the following:

"He who strikes a man so that he dies will surely be put to death.
But, if he did not lie in wait for him but, [he] falls into his hands,
then I will appoint a place to which he may flee.
If however a man acts presumptuously against his neighbor, so as
to kill him craftily, you are to take him even from my altar, that
he may die."

This distinguishes between murder and the lesser crime of manslaughter. The standard taken from this text is used throughout the courtrooms of the U.S. and Canada to this day to differentiate degrees of murder. The difference, interestingly, lies in the intent of the heart, which Jesus addresses so clearly in the Sermon on the Mount.

In one case, a quarrel breaks out, tempers flare, and in the ensuing altercation a person gets killed. Neither party set out to intentionally kill the other, but in the heat of the moment it happened. This is the crime of manslaughter and does not require the penalty of execution. In the other case, the person has conceived of a plan to kill someone, then goes about doing the deed. It is premeditated. There is a bitterness and a hatred that wants to harm the other person. The anger grows and grows in the heart until the opportunity comes to do something about it. This is the definition of murder. The heart motive is the key issue.

THE HEART ATTITUDE DETERMINES THE CRIME

Now we get to the core of this Commandment and how it affects *us* directly. Since the true crime is established by the heart attitude, what happens if we have the heart attitude of wishing someone would drop dead but never have the nerve or opportunity to really kill the person? That is precisely the scenario that Jesus addresses in the Sermon on the Mount. He says we are guilty before the law if we have hatred towards someone even if we don't kill them.

> *"For I say to you that unless your righteousness surpasses that of*
> *the scribes you shall not enter the kingdom of Heaven.*
> *You have heard that the ancients were told, 'You shall not*
> *commit murder' and 'Whoever commits murder will be liable*
> *to the court, but I say to you that everyone who is angry with*
> *his brother shall be guilty before the court, and whoever shall*
> *say to his brother 'you are good for nothing' shall be guilty*
> *before the supreme court and whoever shall say 'you fool'*
> *shall be guilty enough to go into the fiery hell." Matt. 5:20-22*

Jesus said every sin flows out of the heart so what is in our heart is very important to Him. *To God, what we think is the same as what we do.* "Man looks on the outward appearance but God looks at the heart." [1 Samuel 16:7] So it is that while we might look around and see a room full of well dressed, pleasant people, God sees all that is in our hearts! Now it comes home to us. If we take inventory of the thoughts of our heart over the last week, what will we find? Jesus gives His explanation of murder and it consists of the meditation of the heart. He says not to think your brother is a fool. Don't think it because it is the same as the crime of murder. Premeditated murder means that you harbor evil thoughts towards someone then hurt him. In contrast is manslaughter where it happens without holding a hatred towards the person. The only difference is the attitude of the heart. *So the real sin is harboring evil thoughts towards your neighbor. Therefore we enter into the spirit of the sin of murder whenever we hold hatred or anger in our thoughts.* It is something that grows and grows and consumes us even if we don't carry out any hurtful behavior. Something interesting to consider is this; if we have an angry outburst, as most of us do from time to time, have we committed murder? That's a good question. The sin is again determined by the heart attitude. If something annoying happens and we snap at someone, no it isn't the sin of murder, it's actually more akin to manslaughter. It wasn't premeditated, it just happened in the irritation of the moment. It still needs to be repented of quickly because it is a sin. We should keep short accounts and apologize immediately. However if we hold onto anger and it grows into resentment and bitterness; if we allow the angry thoughts to take root without repenting of them, yes, we are then committing the sin of murder. With that said it's now easy to see that we can be murdering somebody all day long even if we are miles away from the one we are angry with!

IT'S SO EASY TO BREAK THIS LAW

For the most part, like the First Commandment -"You shall have no false gods before Me," we feel like we at least have this commandment under control. We feel pretty good since we are confident that we have never killed anyone. But contrary to our high esteem of our own virtue, we probably break this law more than all others except for the first! Let's consider the following:

We travel along our Christian path fairly smoothly. We are upstanding and friendly. We content ourselves that we like people and are likable and therefore we are fulfilling Jesus' command to love God and neighbor. That is, until someone wrongs us. The moment we are crossed watch out! Suddenly we are righteously indignant! We are convinced of our innocence. We are incensed that our rights have been infringed upon! If we are not able to 'set things right' by blasting the person it burns down deep into us. Carnal Christians we are - all love on the outside but bitterly protective of self on the inside. If we are wronged in any way, we lash out with severity. Nor does it have to be a major attack! It can be something as tiny as a look we perceive to be slighting us. It might not even exist except in our minds, but it doesn't matter.

It infects us and pollutes us with the sin of murder. Of course, our enemy wants to make this as easy as possible for us. He's delighting in the wake of destruction that will follow. Working with our own fallen nature, he bombards us with feelings of anger and resentment.

How lucky we are to live today! In centuries gone by the church would have instructed us to die to self, to let it go and to forgive our enemies. That would have been painful and unpleasant. But today we can go to the church and attend a seminar or go to a counsellor who will instruct us on our *right* to be angry! We will be given a complete arsenal of weapons to use against the offending party. If it is a husband, by all means, if he has hurt you in any way, get rid of him! The marriage contract means nothing if your rights are being violated!

So our modern society and our modern church encourage the very anger and resentment that in times past would have been identified as sin. As these feelings are allowed to grow and fester they become the polluting springs of the swamp of murder. So we see that the sin of murder is rampant in society, rampant in the church, and rampant in us!

THE RAMBO EFFECT

Adding to this we have the highly volatile rocket fuel of Hollywood being poured onto our fire. In every movie there must be a villain in order to make a good plot. The aspiration of Hollywood is to make the audience loath the villain to such a degree that they are delighted to see him [or her] blown to pieces in the end. This is stock for action movies as well as drama but also plays into romantic comedies where the intent is to pay it out to the bad guy in the end. We, the audience, are supposed to identify with the hero and enter his own rage against the enemy. I call it the Rambo effect because it is so clearly seen in that movie. For the most part, and especially in that movie, they are very successful in their craft. The audience really does want to be right alongside the hero blasting away at the inhuman Communist torturers and the deceitful American commanders. It seems to be overwhelmingly the right thing to do. But what seems to be gratifying, raw human emotion against supreme injustice actually falls into another category with God. *That category is murder.*

LOVE THY ENEMIES

79

But wait. Didn't we already conclude that killing is allowable under the condition of war? Yes it is. Then how come it's murder in a case like this? Because Jesus said *"love your enemies."* [Matt. 5:44] How do those fit together? Easy! We are to love our enemies even if our duty lies in fighting against them and even in killing them. We are to do our duty, but we are to take no pleasure in doing that duty. We are to have the mind of God in the matter. The Lord God takes no pleasure in punishing evil deeds. He takes no delight in sentencing even the most wicked to hell. He does what He must to maintain justice in the universe. In this way we can see a small reflection of His nature in that of a loving parent. No matter what the child has done the true parent is never anything but sorrowful to have to punish.

Interestingly as you look over the battlefields of history, you will see that the generals and the fighting men that God has blessed and raised up to honor are those who did their job without entering into a spirit of hatred towards the enemy! That is because they have killed without entering the sin of murder. They have kept their heart motivation free of hatred. Those who use their hatred to fuel their attack are inevitably destroyed. They have entered the spirit of murder and have killed because they wanted to. Even those who are being tortured are required to maintain a loving demeanor towards their persecutors. God is strict in regard to His people. He does not want His people to enter the spirit of murder under any circumstances. Jesus requires us to *"be perfect even as our Father in Heaven is perfect."* [Matt. 5:48]

MURDER IN SPORTS

As we consider these things and apply them to our sports we find that the spirit of murder is rampant on the fields. From peewee hocky and little league to high school and college sports we find that winning is everything. In an effort to pump up the team and get more out of them many times the atheletes are coached to foster a spirit of anger towards their opponents. It's that desire to 'kill' the other team that is precisely what is being addressed in this commandment! Gone are the days of sportsmanship where the goal was skill and camaraderie. Now we cultivate a violent desire to annihilate the 'enemy' in our all consuming drive to 'win.' Interestly, in the field of sports as well as on the battlefield it's those who don't enter into that mentality that do well and are blessed by God. So many of the best atheletes are those who practice good sportsmanship towards their rivals instead of hating them. God Himself often elevates them to prominence! It's tragic to see how many pro atheletes have adopted the kill-the-enemy persona. Not only does it kill the game, it kills their souls and the souls of the many kids who emulate them. If we extend this to include the heart attitude of those who are *watching* the game it's clear that the spirit of murder prevails in our society. Have you ever watched parents at a grammar school game? Have you ever watched your own feelings toward a rival team while watching the big game? It's scary in light of the scriptures.

THE SPIRIT OF MURDER PREVAILS

Now to get back to Hollywood. What we see here is a full scale attempt to get the audience to empathize with the hero and so enter the spirit of murder. Their idea is to work hard to bring that particular emotion out and then cause it to grow and envelop the viewer. So now, whenever we personally are caught up in that spirit of a movie, we

have indeed entered the sin of murder and need to repent earnestly before God. That type of anger is *not* of God no matter how justified it seems in the emotion of the moment. We need to steer clear of that type of movie alto- gether because we are no match for the overpowering skills of the movie industry. They will win and they will infect your soul. That is why with the pursuit of personal revival we emphasize the importance of abstaining from worldly movies. They corrupt in ways you don't even know about!

The murderous attitude of our favorite heroes also affects our gen- eral world view. It is very easy to slip into that attitude when someone we esteem paves the way. And so our schools and homes are filled with little copies of heroes who rage against their enemies.Those who want to inherit eternal life must work hard to separate themselves from the prevailing winds of unacceptable behavior. Jesus Himself will be the judge and He said that even calling your brother a fool, without repenting, will result in the penalty of hell.

BLESSED ARE THE PEACEMAKERS

Jesus instructed us that the greatest commandment is to love the Lord and love our neighbor as ourselves. So we must remember that our enemy, the devil, is always trying to stir up anger and incite conflicts. Our job is to refuse. I love the title from an old movie "What If They Gave A War And Nobody Came?" The concept is both funny and intriguing. What if the devil stirred up a conflict and you refused to participate in it? Here is the freedom of Christ! If someone demands that you walk a mile carrying their gear, walk with him two. We don't have to demand our rights! In Jesus we are free to have our rights trampled! We are free from having to get even! Jesus Himself will repay us any injury. In the story of Joseph found in the book of Genesis, his brothers hated him and mightily harmed him by selling him into slavery. Joseph bore all the abuse and injustice quietly and patiently. His time of suffering continued for a long period, and yet he faithfully entrusted his cause to God. In the end Joseph had an opportunity to confront those same brothers, this time as the ruler of Egypt! While the brothers were quaking with fear Joseph comforted them and told them: [Gen. 50:19-20]

> *"Do not be afraid, for am I in God's place? As for you, you meant evil against me, but God meant it for good in order to bring about this present result, to preserve many people alive."*

We can see from this example that we don't have to worry about the consequences of someone wronging us. Our command is to love them and pray for them, knowing that we also offend many and are full of various sins. God wants us to love those who despitefully use us.

 We turn to the cross. Jesus is not just telling us to do these things; He lived it out for us! Imagine enduring the hatred and abuse of those who crucified Him. Yet His last words were *"Father forgive them, for they know not what they do." [Luke 23:34*

LESSON 14

THE SEVENTH COMMANDMENT

THOU SHALT NOT COMMIT ADULTERY

The enemy of our souls is never outright in his purposes against us but rather leads us by degrees into a lifestyle which is contrary to God. And so a society which would have never accepted sexually explicit media only a few decades ago now finds no limit to what is acceptable. In fact the only requirement now is that it sells. That could never have happened if it came about all at once. But because it came by degrees, we now find that what was repulsive only a few years ago is now greeted without even a raised eyebrow. If you, as a Christian, remember what would have seriously bothered your conscience in movie content only ten years ago, you will find that it no longer bothers you. Why? Because ten years of steady viewing has had the effect of conditioning you to accept these things as normal. Now everyone who watches TV or movies, Christian or not, will see on screen that the normal course for meeting someone is to sleep with them that same night. If the characters are lovable and funny and there is no obvious nudity it slips by as an innocent romantic comedy or wholesome family entertainment! These movies fill the homes of church-going Christians. What is acceptable to man is not acceptable to God.

"DO NOT FOLLOW THE MULTITUDE IN DOING EVIL"

What the movies don't portray is the awesome, devastating consequences that inevitably follow the sins of adultery and fornication. Not only do they produce horrible discord, fighting, broken hearts, broken homes, and devastated children, they also incur the strict discipline of the Lord. Each time someone commits a sexual sin an inescapable punishment is sent to them. The penalty is so terrible that they will wish they had never allowed themselves to stray.

Meanwhile, our enemy is bent double with glee. While hiding the true consequences from the naive, he has succeeded in convincing the world that it is very desirable and acceptable to behave in such a manner. Let's see what God's Word has to say on the matter.

Scriptures dealing with sexual sin are truly frightening. Consider just these few,

"Keep your way far from her [the adulteress] and do not go near her door.
Lest you give your years to the cruel one and you groan at your latter end, when your flesh and body are consumed."

"He will be held with the cords of his sin. He will die for lack of instruction." Proverbs 5:8-23

"Can a man take fire into his heart and not be burned?
So is the one who goes in to his neighbors wife.
Whoever goes in to her will not go unpunished." Prov. 6:27-29

"With her many persuasions she entices him, with her flattering lips she seduces him.
Suddenly he follows her as an ox goes to the slaughter.
Until an arrow pierces through his liver.
As a bird hastens to the snare, so he does not know it will cost him his life." Prov. 7:21-23

"Do not let your heart turn aside to her ways, do not stray into her paths.
For many are the victims she has cast down and numerous are her slain.
Her house is the way to Sheol, descending to the chambers of death." Prov. 7:25-27

"If my heart has been enticed by a woman,
that would be a lustful crime, moreover it would be an iniquity punishable by judges.
For it would be fire that consumes to Abaddon [hell]
and would uproot all my increase." Job 31:9 -12

Perhaps most serious of all is the verse found in Malachi 2:14 -15

"The Lord has been a witness between you and the wife of your
youth, against whom you have dealt treacherously, though she
is your companion and your wife by covenant.
Not one has done so who has a remnant of the Spirit."

We see that contrary to public opinion, the punishment for sins of
the flesh are extreme! Rather than us excusing them because they are so
prevalent in us and society, we must learn to *fear* breaking the Seventh
Commandment. Sexual immorality is one of the sins which we are *not*
instructed to stand firm against. Rather we are instructed to flee!
   "Flee immorality. Every other sin a man commits is outside the
   body, but the immoral man sins against his own body."
   1 Cor. 6:18.

GRIEVING THE HOLY SPIRIT

Who can imagine anything more fearful than what is described
above where God says "not one has done so [engaged in immoral be-
havior] who has a remant of the Spirit? With our overemphasis today on
the love of God we find that many sins which God mightily condemns
are glossed over by the church at large. Professing church members
and pastors can engage in immorality only to be quickly excused by
'God's love and forgiveness.' As mentioned earlier, we can indeed be
forgiven if we heartily repent, but the consequences of sin remain. A
wake of destruction will follow those who fall into adulterous sin no
matter who they are or how the sin is passed over by the congrega-
tion. Worst of all, what cannot be detected by man may happen to us.
If we treat it lightly, we may grieve the Holy Spirit. When that occurs
a blindness sets in that prevents us from realizing it. So we can go on
confidently thinking that all we do is wonderful in the sight of God
when in fact, we have grieved the Holy Spirit!
[Ephesians 4:30]. *Of this we can be sure, there*
is not a single false prophet in this age or any
other that realizes they are a false prophet.
Each one is completely right in his own eyes
and firmly convinced of his standing with
God. Such is the nature of sin. Consider the
confirmation of this in Psalm 36: 1-2.

Thus Sayeth the LORD!

"Transgression speaks to the ungodly within his heart, there is no fear of God before his eyes.
For it flatters him in his own eyes, concerning the discovery of his iniquity and the hatred of it."

If there is unconfessed, unforsaken sin in the life of a church leader, no matter how popular they are with men, God will say "I never knew you." That is why the instruction must be to fear and run from sin.

WHY IS IT SO WRONG?

God made man and woman as majestic creatures. The scripture says, 'He made man only a little lower than angels.' God made mankind to be full of wisdom, holiness, beauty, intelligence and talents. He made them to become, as His sons and daughters, just like Him. We have actually been given a new spiritual genetic code when we receive His Holy Spirit. It shapes us and causes us to develop in a Godly direction.

As part of that new spiritual being He included one area dealing with sex. Within the context of our complete person it is also wonderful if it is in God. But no matter how wonderful that area may be, God created us to be noble creatures growing into things higher and better than sex. God wants to elevate men and women. He wants them to control their passions in sex as in every other area and use it within the legally defined boundaries. When it is used properly, it even becomes a true form of genuine love. Genuine love consists of thinking of the other person rather than yourself. That translated to physical love makes it a beautiful and unselfish act. Love is the unselfish attempt to please the other person.

Lust on the other hand is the animal desire to gratify your own needs. So while God seeks to elevate men and women to where His love is brought even into the realm of sex, the enemy of mankind works to do the opposite. Remember his goal is to get us to break all the commandments. So he works at building lust. His desire is to make passions rise so that everyone becomes the object of lust. He wants to reduce the noble creature God made to *only* passions. He wants to reduce God's supreme creation into animal lust of the lowest form. So instead of being creatures controlled by reason and love they become even lower than the animals by elevating their passion for sex into the whole of their existence. Satan constantly stirs up lust so that instead of being a society of people made in God's image, capable of glorious harmony, we are reduced to a society of objects. We no longer interact with each other as people but are only interested in what we can get.

LUST IS THE OPPOSITE OF LOVE

Lust is the opposite of love and since God is love it is also the opposite of God. The two are mutually exclusive. To try to enjoy the gift of sex without love or God is impossible. Since God is the author and creator of sex, when He is left out, it becomes empty and completely unsatisfying. Why do so many women have to 'fake' their enjoyment? Because it's not satisfying. Why is it not satisfying? Love and its Author have been left out. This is one of those built in penalties that abound in the universe.

C.S. Lewis deals with this subject handily. He explains that the devil's way is to fill us with lust by giving us a taste of something sinful. Then the more the lust increases the less gratification he gives. It's called the 'law of diminishing returns.' The more you indulge in lust the less satisfying it becomes. The devil's glory is to get humans to the point where they are all lust with no gratification. Then they are in hell. Lewis says the very fires of hell will be burning passions with no gratification. So the devil goes about his work tempting the whole world with endless longings for people they shouldn't be with. He makes it

 an overwhelming desire, he make it intoxicating. He doesn't let anyone see the real consequences which always follow. He tries to cover up the broken homes, multiple mothers and fathers, the endless fights and abuse. But most of all he doesn't want anyone to know ahead of time that they are trading it all for nothing! There will be no gratification in the lustful relationship. It is an illusion, nothing more, nothing less, that is deceiving us.

On the other side is something wonderful and humorous. That is, where God is present, the physical relationship of a man and wife is satisfying beyond anything the world has ever dreamed of! So the heated passion displayed on the screen is in fact only acting, but real Godly romance is found in the most unassuming of homes! The little Godly housewife, that the world would never look twice at, will often  enjoy supreme heights of satisfaction while the world would look on with envy if they knew. I love how God does that. The satisfaction in the relationship comes from the true love which is demonstrated by loving and enjoying the pleasure you are giving your spouse, something which lust simply cannot do! God's blessing is on faithful marriages and He rewards them in all ways, including the area of physical love. The thrill is not in an extramarital affair, it's in carefully cultivating love in marriage!

It's disturbing to find much teaching in the church today that actully encourages lust in marriage. The reasoning is that if it's within the context of marriage anything goes. That is not true. Lust is the opposite of love and destroys love. As we go into a marriage relationship and carry our lustful thoughts and behavior into it we will invariably bring great hurt and heartbreak to our spouse. The lustful relationship will not stand because lust is selfishness in it's purest [or most impure] form. Avoid lust at all cost, pursue love. That is the quickest way to having a fulfilling relationship!

To be pitied most are those who go from one lustful relationship to another with no commitment. They are in the final stages before hell. They are desperately seeking the thrill of lust but it eludes them. With each new partner the satisfaction is less and less and as they get older it becomes truly pathetic.

LESSON 15

THE ATOMS OF SOCIETY

God's building block for the material universe is the atom. The atom is not the smallest particle, but it is the smallest unit. Everything we see is constructed on the foundation of atoms. As tiny as they are, if they suddenly flew apart, the universe would dissolve!

When God built His crown of life, mankind, He used the same principle. The smallest unit in the universe of people is the family. Everything else is constructed out of that building block. As tiny as the individual family is, if it should fly apart all of society would dissolve. It is the smallest unit and it was not meant to be split. Just like atoms, they weren't meant to be tampered with. When man goes into the material world and splits what God joined together, immense destruction results. Men try to harness it, but they are trying to harness the power of destruction and the consequences are grave, even to the annihilation of the planet.

So also when men split the family which God ordained in marriage, tremendous devastation comes forth. Even if on the surface things appear to be not so bad, there are invisible consequences. Just like radiation, you can't see it but it's given off when atoms are split and causes cancer and death. With families it is the same. Splitting families exposes them to harmful radiation which causes death and deformity. From there it radiates into all of society. That's why adultery was punished by death in the Old Testament. The results in the people are so terrible that God wanted to protect His beloved creation.

JESUS' DEFINITION

Jesus, of course, went far beyond the pharisee's approach to the matter. He knew that to protect the family it would take much more than outward compliance to laws prohibiting the act of adultery. He knew and taught that all bad actions are the result of first thinking bad thoughts. This is summed up in the words of James 1:14 -16;

"But each one is tempted when he is carried away and enticed by his own lust [thoughts].
Then when lust has conceived it gives birth to sin, and when sin is accomplished it brings forth death.
Do not be deceived my beloved brethren."

So Jesus aimed at the heart of sin which originates in the thoughts of men and women. Consider His expansion of this Commandment;

"You have heard it said 'You shall not commit adultery'
But I say that everyone who looks on a woman to lust for her has committed adultery with her already in his heart.
And if your right eye makes you stumble, tear it out, and throw it from you;
For it is better for you that one of the parts of your body perish, than for your whole body to be thrown in hell." Matt. 5: 27-29

UNFAITHFUL THOUGHTS

As with the sin of murder, to God, what you think is the same as what you do. He said that not only were we not to be unfaithful, we were not even to have unfaithful thoughts. Why is that so important? There are two reasons. First, the seeds of adultery are planted when

 husbands and wives look at someone else as though they were attractive. The human mind acts just like a garden. Whatever seed is put in it grows into a plant. It is the law of nature and the scripture addresses it saying,
"Do not be deceived my beloved brethren for whatever a man sows that will he also reap." Gal. 6:7

What enters into the mind, unless it is vigorously resisted, will come to pass. A person who allows adulterous thoughts to be in his mind will end up in adultery. Second, the bond of the family is love. God is love and He is the glue. Just like atoms are held together by God with no other explanation, so is the family. His love makes the unit of the family hold together. When a spouse looks at another person in such a way as to desire him or her, it is an unspeakable crime against love - God's and the other spouse's. If a woman who loves her husband with her whole heart finds that he is desiring to be with another person, that wife's heart will be devastated! It doesn't matter one bit that he didn't actually cheat on her. The fact that he desired to is just as bad to her. The husband who fully trusts in the love of his bride will be destroyed if he learns she's been thinking lustful thoughts about another man.

ROMANTIC BOOKS AND MOVIES

On that subject have you ever noticed that magazines, movies and books all focus on true love being in the spontaneous passion that arises from a chance encounter with a stranger or a co-worker? Old relationships are dumped in the pursuit of this new 'true romance.' Have you ever wondered what it feels like to be on the other side of that, to be the partner who is thrown out after years of devotion, for a passing kiss? That stray look, that stray lustful glance, that chance encounter is your death. That seed will come back to you and the life you destroy by leaving your thoughts unbridled will end up being yours! It will pursue you and overtake you like the angel of death. Run and be afraid. Adulterous thoughts are the doorway to hell. Avoid every movie and every magazine that will make it seem attractive. It will be your life you save as well as your spouse and your children.

TO ADULTERATE

Interestingly, the definition of adulterate is 'to make lower in quality by adding inferior or improper materials.' While we consider making our lives more exciting by adding a new romantic element, we are in fact lowering or adulterating the quality of our life.

Because of the tremendous pressure put on families today by our lust-driven society, these sins, adultery and fornication, will be your greatest temptation and your greatest possibility of falling away from Jesus. There is no married man or woman who does not face these temptations continually and each must be determined to fight them off as though their very lives depended on it. It does.

WORKING FOR THE DEVIL

Here is something else to consider. We know that the devil is constantly trying to stir up lust in order to separate us from God and harvest our souls. For as much as we ourselves cause someone to stumble because of our behavior or dress, we are joining in the devil's work of luring a soul onto the rocks. Whenever we dress or act in a manner to cause someone to stumble we unwittingly become a tool of the devil. That's not a very pleasant thought, is it? And don't doubt that you can be an instrument of evil. Jesus called His best friend a devil for tempting Him to go against God's will. And so we are commanded by scripture to act in a manner that is becoming to a child of God and appropriate to those around us.

MODESTY, THE FORGOTTEN VIRTUE

To be attractive, which is deemed the highest good in modern society, has become synonymous with being provocative. That rule follows all social levels and all fields of employment no matter how loudly they protest. But God would have His people to be peculiar people. He would have them aspire to a completely different standard. He would have them to be so completely odd that they would stand out as anomalies in our modern society. That is all accomplished in just one word, *modesty*. The very word is lost today. What was once considered a high virtue is now virtually unknown. A citizen of a century ago who had the misfortune of being transported to our time would consider the world had gone mad because all the women had become prostitutes! The ordinary clothing worn in schools and public places reflects an immodesty once reserved only for hookers. That is really something to consider. What we see now as commonplace is not only totally against the precepts of God, but it would be considered totally unacceptable by nearly every society through history! Even barbaric cultures of the past had enough concern for their women to not let them flaunt their sexuality. The most pagan cultures had enough sense not to parade their young girls about in such a fashion as to provoke unbridled lust. They knew it would destroy their civilization. Read history, don't take my word for it.

God would have His people to be modest. He would have modesty in their clothing, modesty in their behavior and modesty in their words. How do we define modest? Anything that could stir up lust is immodest.

"Likewise, I want women to adorn themselves with proper clothing, modestly and discreetly by means of good works, as befits women who make a claim to godliness." 1 Timothy 2: 9-10

NO EXCUSE

Forgive me if this sounds a bit one-sided but, in many ways, this seems to apply especially to women. One of the most common excuses I hear for immodest dress is "I'm not attractive, what I wear won't bother anyone." That is not true. You have no idea what another might consider provocative. It is also well known that many women are self conscious and don't consider themselves sexy. That becomes the driving force in their dress. This is a trap that is very difficult to get out of. But, you are responsible before God not to lead someone into sinful thoughts. Men are easily, very easily, led in that direction and, of course, if you are honest, you enjoy the attention! You must work hard not to be on satan's team leading someone astray. You say it's their fault? God is the judge. Be careful.

Anyone can dress immodestly. Anyone can flaunt their sexuality. Only a child of God can dress modestly. It requires going out of your way. You must be inconvenienced to dress modestly. You know in the normal stores you will find only the latest, most immodest clothing. It is a courageous and special child who forsakes the world to please her truest love. Go out of your way. God has called us to be holy and has given us His Spirit to help us.

93

Those who embrace His cross and join Him in death to self will also be joined with Him in the glory of His resurrection! Halleluia!

MODESTY IN SPEECH

We must be modest in our speech. We must not copy the world by letting perverted words out of our mouths. Nor should we laugh at jokes or mention things that are sexually charged. This becomes a serious exercise for some who enter easily into worldly conversations. Here again is the strength and comfort of fellowship. To know there are others who are persevering in this area is a great help.

"Let no unwholesome word proceed from your mouth, but only
such a word as is good for edification according to the need of
the moment, that it may give grace to those who hear."
Ephesians 4: 29.

This is a key tenet of God's word to direct us in our conversation. It's not a suggestion, it's God's command to us. Immodest speech is completely inappropriate and unacceptable for His children.

THE SWITCH

One of the scariest things to remember is that our enemy who is *all lust* is able to manipulate our emotions to such a degree that it's as though he has a switch that turns on our attractions. So it is common to experience an overwhelming magnetic pull towards someone who we should not be with. We find it's so hard to resist the temptation. Is this the real, passionate love we have always been longing for? It sure feels like it! As we give in and sever our family ties in our pursuit of 'true love' an interesting thing happens. After we've caused irreparable damage and broken our vows and gone with the new lover, guess what? The same one who lured us to destroy our family now simply clicks the switch again, *off.* Now the passionate attraction evaporates! We can't imagine how we were ever attracted to them! So we find we have traded everything precious and many times even our eternal life for nothing, just a handful of sand. We become like Esau who despised his birthright and sold his inheritance for a single meal. Selah.

LESSON 16

THE CAMP OF THE CANAANITES

"The people began to play the harlot with the daughters of Moab."

God spoke clearly to His people that He did not want them to mix with the inhabitants of the land. He promised severe punishments to those who defiled themselves with their immorality. He told them to be separate and not go near those who would pollute them with uncleanness. Today we serve the same God who demands purity in His people.

But there is a difference for us today. In the days of Moses, the Israelites 'went out to visit the daughters of the land.' Today we needn't take so much trouble, the inhabitants of the land come to us! The very sin, which was unbridled passion, is now at our doorstep and right within our home. Gross immorality which defies description is now pumped right into our living rooms and offices via internet, TV and movies. It is almost inescapable in it's pervasiveness. Those who may have led moral lives only a few decades ago are now corrupted by the constant bombardment of sexually explicit input. That corruption causes incalculable damage to marriages, children and society.

There is no middle ground now. There is no place now for 'decent people' that do not know the Savior. Those who desire to be clean, must seek it with all their might. Those who want to be faithful to their spouses must now be aggressive in their pursuit of it. They must want it as though it was a matter of life and death, because it is. We must willfully seek purity of heart and mind. We call it 'willful innocence.' It is actively striving to become blameless, innocent children of God. As children we have a naive innocence about us but as we grow up in this society all trace of innocence is lost. But God has made a way to regain that purity again. It is only for those who earnestly repent and call to God for help that help is given. Those who *'seek will find'* and obtain the precious treasure of willful innocence.

The sexual perversion and animal lust which is now only a click away is like having a window into the very camp of the Canaanites. That window is easily opened because it can be viewed with the feeling of complete anonymnity. What we don't know is that God's camera of eternity is taping every episode and it will be played back at a very awkward moment. What once took active seeking is now placed right at the finger tips of every husband, family man and young man. Making things worse is that it solicits like the harlot mentioned in Proverbs 7. It comes to get us. It is alluring and seductive, almost impossible to get away from.

Almost is the key. With every temptation God provides a way out. Those who seek life must seek it with all their strength and all their might. They must be determined that they don't want to die and must pray with all earnestness. Like the harlot in Proverbs, sexual sin *"Lurks at every corner, she seizes him and kisses him."* The immorality of the world is not sitting by passively, it is actively seeking new victims to devour. *"For many are the victims she has cast down, and numerous are her slain. Her house is the way to hell."* Prov. 7:26-27

HOW DO I GET OUT?

I hope this terrifies you, because it is only those who are terrified who will make the effort necessary to escape the grip of this sin. For those whose awakened consciences are burning and wanting to be right with God, there are these helps;

First, there is no way out until we realize we are utterly, hopelessly trapped with no way to escape. If you are not yet convinced of this just simply try to live the next week without any sexual sin! Most of us, however are painfully aware of how impossible that is. So the first step is to openly and honestly confess the sin to the Father. Do not hold back any detail [He knows them already]. Admit before Him and yourself that there is no righteousness whatever in you and that you are desperate for His help. If you side-step the issue because of your desire to continue in hidden sin, and simply try to do a little better, no help will come to you. You must see the consequence of sin is death and pray fervently with that in mind.

Second, you will find great help by praying for God to take away your *desire* for sexual sin. Tell Him openly that your fallen nature craves those things and that you can't even be sincere in asking Him to remove them from your life. Then tell Him you are willing but that you need a true desire to be free. Ask Him to give you a desire to *want* to be good. Honestly acknowledging that you can't stop because you desire to sin will put God on your side. He will send a double portion of strength of His Spirit to those who are bound with the cords of sin and cry out for freedom! You will really find amazing things happen after praying like that. Sexual sin will become repulsive to you. He will help you see it in its true light. You'll see that it's ugly and empty. A wonderful verse to repeat out loud to find relief is Psalms 124:7-8;

"Our soul has escaped like a bird out of the snare of the trapper,
   The snare is broken and we have escaped.
Our help is in the name of the Lord who made heaven and
   earth."

Third, begin to take practical steps to avoid sin. It is not enough to say "The Lord will have to do it because I can't." He also requires action. Faith without works is dead. Proverbs 4 and 5 say this,
   "Do not enter the path of the wicked, and do not proceed in the
      way of evil men.
   Avoid it, do not pass by. Turn away from it and pass on."

"Keep your way far from her, [immorality]
   and do not go near the door of her house."

If that means disconnecting your cable, call them today! Halleluia! If that means throwing out your TV, so be it! You have others here who have taken the commitment with you. You will find fellowship in Christ to be infinitely more stimulating! What about the worst temptation of all, the internet? You say you can't live without it. Amazingly, higher forms of civilization have existed for thousands of years without it. Men have reached great heights of art, science, philosophy and religion all without the aid of the internet! If for some reason [such as your job] you find it necessary to keep your link, do this; join with others who are seeking to have a consecrated life and install software which screens sexual content. Let each one install it for his brother so that each password is only known by someone else. It is a bold step that will cause your Father delight!

Fourth, pray early. Do everything in your power to avoid a situation that you know will make you fall, but prayer before you start to be tempted will be the most effective way to

accomplish this. Once you feel the powerful magnet of sex attracting you it is almost a lost cause. Your fallen human nature will almost certainly win that battle; you will give in and then find yourself miserable again for days as you feel yourself separated from God. So you must pray before the spell is upon you, while you are still in a godly state of mind. Earnestly beseech God in the morning to help you avoid sin and to give you a shield of purity. Ask Him to make you pure in spirit. Ask Him to give you purity of eye and purity of heart. You will find true supernatural help. God takes pleasure in those simple honest prayers and knows you can't do it yourself.

That's why Jesus came! He came to be our purity before God and then to impart His purity to us! Remember when we receive His precious Spirit, with Him comes a new genetic code, a code that will eventually make us beautiful and clean. We will become like Him, the First of many brothers, because it is promised that *"He who began a good work in us will be faithful to complete it." Phil. 1:6*

To further emphasize the importance of praying early, we see the model for it in the Lord's Prayer. It says 'Lead us not into temptation, but deliver us from evil.' Jesus knowing our nature as He did, had no delusions of the strength of human character and therefore urges us to pray early. He says to ask God for help to avoid temptation. That is a lot different than the halfhearted prayers that come once we are in the magnetic pull of sin! Earnest prayer while you are in God's presence will certainly bring results.

Fifth, imagine what it would be like if a specially designed monitor were strapped to your head that displayed for all the world, every thought that ran through your mind! That would make you careful, wouldn't it? Well, unfortunately for us, God has already invented that technology. Every thought of our minds is clearly and openly visible to Him! He knows every thought and intent

of the heart. Our innermost parts are laid bare before Him. Since the Lord considers what we think to be equivalent to what we do, this should make us very careful! It is a sobering realization and helps us to monitor our thought life.

MORE SCRIPTURAL WARNINGS

Here are more passages dealing with the area of immorality;
"Or do you not know that the unrighteous will not inherit the
*   kingdom of God? Do not be decieved, neither fornicators,*
*   nor idolaters, nor adulterers, nor effeminate,*
*   nor homosexuals." 1 Cor. 6:9*

"But do not let any immorality or any impurity or greed even be
*   named among you as is proper for saints.*
And there must be no filthiness or coarse jesting, which are not
*   fitting, but rather the giving of thanks.*
For this you know with certainty, that no immoral or impure
*   person or covetous man, who is an idolater, has an inheritance*
*   in the kingdom of Christ and God.*
Let no one deceive you with empty words, for because of these
*   things the wrath of God comes upon the sons of disobedience."*
Ephesians 5: 3 - 6

"For this is the will of God, your sanctification, that you abstain
*   from sexual immorality.*
"And let no man transgress and defraud his brother in the matter
*   because the Lord is the avenger in all these things just as we*

told you and solemnly warned you.
For God has not called us for the purpose of impurity but in
*   sanctification." 1 Thes. 4:3-7*

HELP FOR THOSE ALREADY DEVASTATED BY ADULTERY

If perhaps you are one of the many unfortunates who have already fallen to temptation and reaped the bitter consequences of adultery, what hope is there for you? For starters read through this lesson again and begin from this moment to practice the precepts of God in your daily life. It is very important for you to realize that God's purpose in creating you was to make you a good, obedient child. Many, many have learned hard lessons by sowing sin and reaping the whirlwind. If that harvest of corruption causes you to hate and fear sin, then God will turn even sin itself into His servant. Remember it was Mary Magdalene that was the first person Jesus appeared to. He also gave us the hope of saying *"He that is forgiven much loveth much." Luke 7:36-50*

Many of the great men of the Bible have sinned in grievous ways. It has the wonderful effect of producing real humility and dependance upon God. In some people it's a lesson that can't be learned any other way. Don't get me wrong, you will still have to suffer the results of your sin. King David was called a man after God's own heart and yet when he sinned in adultery, he was punished severely and felt the effects of it for many years. But the important thing is that he was restored to God. Because of his sorrowful repentance God accepted him and loved him and caused even sin to be turned to the good. His son through Bathsheba became the greatest king of Israel and it is his words we read now to deter us from the folly of sexual sin. That is indeed a wonderful promise; *'all things work together for good to those who love God and are called according to His purpose.' [Romans 8:28]* Nothing, absolutely nothing, is outside of that promise. Our loving Savior is able to turn even sin and death and Satan into tools of His mercy. So be of good cheer. Strengthen your feeble knees and begin today to walk in the path of righteousness.

LESSON 17

THE EIGHTH COMMANDMENT

THOU SHALT NOT STEAL

The essence of this commandment is that we would be free from the love of money. Jesus taught about these dangers in Matthew 19: 23 -24.

> *"Truly I say to you it is hard for a rich man to enter the*
> *Kingdom of Heaven.*
> *And again I say to you it is easier for a camel to go through*
> *the eye of a needle than for a rich man to enter the*
> *Kingdom of God."*

What makes these words so inclusive is that you don't have to actually be rich to have a difficult time entering the Kingdom because of money. If we apply the heart attitude to this commandment as Jesus did to the others we see that even if we are poor or middle class and we are filled with a desire for money or are unwilling to part with what we have to follow Him we are very much in danger. He only picks on the rich because they have more to let go of. If the average person clutches to what they have, even if it's only a small amount compared to the wealthy, they are equally in danger of forfeiting the Kingdom of Heaven for material goods. Now this is cause for concern because that includes nearly everyone.

What God is addressing in this commandment is that with freedom from the love of money we are able to steer clear of many of the pitfalls which surround us on all sides. We are like pilgrims wandering through a valley of tarpits. To our left and right and dead ahead are treacherous holes filled with a hot gummy substance which will pull us down to our deaths. That tarry substance is the love of money. Here are some of the things it can do to you once you carelessly slip into it.

BEWARE OF GREED IN ALL ITS FORMS

It makes you greedy. This sin is selfishness in its truest form. It is something which covers us in black tar and makes us exceedingly ugly before God. Jesus said *"Beware, and be on your guard against every form of greed; for not even when one has an abundance does his life consist of his possessions." Luke 12:15.*

Greed is so ugly to God because it is the opposite of His love. Greed is manifested by always wanting the best for yourself without concern for the other person. His love is manifested by wanting the best for the other person even at our own expense. Entering into a greedy mentality you will find it exceedingly difficult to avoid stealing in all its forms. Consider just these few:

RETURNING LOST ITEMS, AN AMAZING STORY

One form of stealing is to find something lost that's desirable to you and don't make an earnest effort to return it. Let me give an interesting example of the type of honesty that God loves and requires. A young man ordered something valuable from a catalog company. It was not for himself, though it was something that he very much would have liked for himself. It was a gift for his brother. When the parcel arrived, amazingly it contained *two* of the items. The second one hadn't even been billed to him; it was a shipping error! There was absolutely no way for the company to find out about the loss. An ordinary person would have simply kept the item without a second thought. But, this was not an ordinary person. This was a young man who was a child of God and a member of the Fellowship of the Unashamed. So he proceeded to call the company to inform them of the error. It didn't stop there! It took him several calls and detailed explanations to convince them of the mistake. When he thought he was finally able to make them understand, he found a month later that they had credited back to his account the full amount of the item! Now he not only had the extra item but also several hundred dollars refunded to his credit card! Again let me remind you that this was not something he couldn't use, but something he really wanted. More phone calls followed and eventually they recharged his card. By this time he decided to keep the item and simply pay for it rather than trying to send it back. The final result was, in reward for his honesty they only charged him half price for the second item. So God blessed Him in the end with a perfectly clear conscience and with the item.

An unusual young man? Perhaps. It made me to be proud to be in the Fellowship of the Unashamed with him! But unusual in the eyes of God? No. He expects all His children to behave in a similar manner. His people must, as in this case, fight to do the honest thing - not just fight, but keep on fighting. He could never have done that if he hadn't been free from the love of money. Because he considered God to be his treasure, earthly things had no hold on him and he was able to do what would have been literally impossible for most people. There is a beautiful verse in Job 22; 24-26. It reads,

"Place your gold in the dust, and the gold of Ophir among the stones of the brook.
Then the Almighty will be your gold and choice silver to you.
For then you will delight in the Almighty and lift up your face to God."

This man had made the Almighty to be his gold and choice silver. Therefore it was possible for him to let go of improper gain and behave in a manner which greatly pleased his earthly and heavenly fathers. What would make this case so difficult to many is the rationalization that 'they hadn't done anything wrong.' That may be true, but we must abide by a higher law. That law is "Do unto others as you would have them do unto you." If you were in business you certainly would not want to mistakenly send out valuable goods for free. Therefore, we are bound to do the right thing.

TAXES

Here's another common cause for stumbling - tax evasion by unreported income. *What the government doesn't know can't hurt them, but it can kill you!* There are literally thousands of ways to hide income and cheat on income tax. All you have to do is ask for cash for a transaction and it is not traceable by the government. What is overlooked is that it is very much traceable by God. He keeps a strict account of everything you do and He will require it of you if you deal dishonestly even with the impersonal, universally-despised government.

There are many who make a sport of trying to cheat the government, and they are cheered on by friends and family. Even some Christian groups fall into this tragic mindset and teach against paying taxes! They fail to realize that the government has been placed over them by God for their protection and good. If the logic were followed to the end and no one paid taxes, you couldn't drive, because there would be no road upkeep. There would be no police, so all you owned would be at the mercy of dishonest men who never paid their taxes! There would be no armed forces, so your country would be at the mercy of any invading army. *Government is merely the organization of the community to provide for the needs that no single person could manage.*

 The government is nothing more than the management of a very large family. When you cheat on taxes you are actually stealing everybody's money. That should make you think of it differently. You get the idea. There is no need to elaborate further. Romans 13:5-8 says,

"Wherefore it is necessary to be in subjection not only because of wrath but also for conscience sake.
For because of this you also pay taxes, for rulers are servants of God, devoting themselves to this very thing.
Render to all what is due them: tax to whom tax is due; custom to whom custom; fear to whom fear; honor to whom honor.
Owe nothing to anyone except to love one another; for he who loves his neighbor has fulfilled the law."

THINK ABOUT THIS

Next time you are presented with an opportunity to cheat the government ask yourself how much is your soul worth. If it's worth more than the amount you're trying to save then you are on the losing end of the deal.

Unfaithfulness in labor is another easy and often hard to detect form of stealing. When we are hired for a job we are expected to work diligently at it. It is not just expected by your boss but also by your Heavenly Boss. Consider the words of Paul in Colossians 3: 23-25;

"Whatever you do, do your work heartily as unto the Lord rather than for men.

Knowing that from the Lord you will receive the reward of the inheritance.

It is the Lord Christ whom you serve.

For he who does wrong will receive the consequences of the wrong which he has done, and that without partiality.

God expects us to work hard and with a good will even if our boss is tough and demanding. Note this same verse begins with an exhortation to slaves to work with all diligence and sincerity of heart, fearing the Lord. This is our freedom in Christ! Those whose focus is their money will never be satisfied. They will always be demanding more, they will always be complaining. Rather than trying to do their job diligently, they are only interested in what they can get. This is a polluting mindset and will make them the type of employee that every boss wants to get rid of!

"He who is slack in his work is brother to him who destroys."
Prov. 18 : 9

If we are free from the love of money, we can do anything for anybody. We can go the extra mile, because we are more concerned with pleasing the customer and our boss than ourselves. When we adopt this godly mindset a wonderful thing starts to happen: *if we work as unto the Lord, the Lord pays us!* God becomes our defender and the source of our income.

God has ordained laws in His universe to protect you. If you are being unfairly treated or underpaid for your work, and yet do it cheerfully unto God, His mechanism kicks in to make sure you receive just compensation. Consider Proverbs 14:23,

"In all labor there is profit."

This is God's promise to us that God will reward our labors. We are free to leave our needs and concerns in His care and He will faithfully watch over us. This promise from His Holy Word will start to operate and you will be blessed. Remember back to Deuteronomy; if you are careful to obey all His precepts all these blessings will pursue you and overtake you. Just don't be weary in well-doing for *'in due season you will reap if you faint not'* Gal. 6:9. Here are just a few examples of God's faithfulness:

THREE EXAMPLES

When the Jews were reduced to slavery during their time in Egypt, they worked long difficult hours without pay. That mistreatment came up before the Lord and He sent Moses to set them free. But before they left the land, God did an amazing thing. He had all the Egyptians give the Jews gold, silver and precious stones as repayment for all their labors. God did not forget! Ex. 12:35, 36

When Jacob worked for his uncle Laban, he was treated unfairly and cheated out of his wages many times. Despite this, he continued serving him without complaint. Finally the time came for him to depart back to the land of Canaan. But before he did, God supernaturally blessed his herds and his flocks so that all his cheated wages were made up!

Right in our own time we have seen the principle demonstrated clearly. When Nazi Germany sought to annihilate the Jews, they first confiscated their property. Many were prosperous merchants, so the plunder was vast. Despite Hitler's plans, God's plan was to free the Jews and give them their own land again. This was accomplished on May 14th, 1948. Fifty years later, when all hope was lost of ever recovering the stolen property, God remembered! God kept track of all earnings that were honestly gained and in the 1990's He began to return it to them and their descendants! How good is God?

If you work hard at honest labor, God Himself will make sure you are rewarded. If you have labored, that money is safer than if it was in the bank.

Another way to steal is to pay honest debts in a slow and grudging manner. When people provide services for us, God expects us to be prompt in paying for those services. Any lack in repayment is stealing, plain and simple. Remember that in any situation where you have received a service from someone and they haven't been paid, God is on *their side*. If you don't have the money, as is often the case, pray earnestly for God to help you take care of the debt. You will be surprised how He will help you. God simply wants you to be honest and concerned about the matter. Don't just let it go and forget about it.

THE EMPLOYER

If you are an employer there are a number of other areas which you will have to be very careful about. If in your quest of profit for yourself you grind your employees down to an unfair wage, you will find yourself contending with God. He may care about you, but He also cares about every one who works for you. He knows their names, where they live and all the hardships they may be enduring right now because of *you!* Consider the words of Job:

"If I have despised the claim of my [employees] when they filed a
complaint against me,
What then could I do when God arises and when He calls me to
account, what answer will I give Him?
Did not He who made me in the womb make him, and the same
one fashion us in the womb?" Job 31: 13 -15

It is important to remember that God is always on the side of the oppressed. If you are treating your people unfairly, their cries will reach the ears of the Almighty. The God of justice will require fair wages of you. He also demands prompt payment. Consider also the words of Leviticus 19:13 and Proverbs 3:27-28

"You shall not oppress your neighbor or rob him.
The wages of a hired man are not to remain with you all night.
"Do not withhold good from those to whom it is due, when it is in
your power to do it.
Do not say, "Go and come back and tomorrow I will give it,"
when you have it with you."

The heart of all God's law is love. If we love those who work for us, we will be glad to give them their wages. We will be happy that we are able to provide work and income for them. Our delight is in caring for others. Job's words are a wonderful reminder that God has placed each one in his position for the good of all. The employer and the employee are the same to Him and He made each one.

USURY

Usury is another area we touched on earlier under the heading of ill-gotten gain. Where the Bible does not prohibit gain through ordinary interest, it does strictly forbid usury. So what is usury? It is charging an unfair interest rate to someone who is in need. It is *using* their circumstances to take advantage of them. Usury, not surprisingly, is very common today and you can read in every investment publication about companies bragging of their exorbitant returns. In almost all cases the return they promise is built on the conscience-free bilking of the naive. Unsuspecting people purchasing on credit will find to their dismay a year later that they have entered the spider's web and can't get out. Their interest rate has gone through the roof without notice and it's impossible to pay down the balance. So month by month the users flog money from these unfortunates. But, there is a God in Heaven, and He is a God of justice. What He says is,

"He who increases his wealth through interest and usury,
Gathers it for him who is gracious to the poor." Prov. 28:8

God will eventually take back all that ill-gotten gain and give it to the oppressed again. He will give it to those who will in turn pass it on to the poor. I love how God does that.

Something to think about is this - you don't have to be the one flogging the poor with excessive rates, *all you have to do is increase your wealth by it*. That means if you personally invest in a company that does that, God will Himself take it back from you! So be careful where you invest and be aware that in almost all cases where you are promised higher than normal returns, someone is being taken advantage of. God will balance the scales.

WILL YOU ROB GOD?

"You are cursed with a curse, for you are robbing Me, the whole
nation of you."
"Bring the whole tithe into the storehouse, so that there may be
food in My house, and test me now in this," says the Lord
of Hosts,
"If I will not open for you the windows of heaven and pour out for
you a blessing until it overflows." Mal. 3:9, 10

There is another form of stealing which is well to avoid, and that
is stealing from God Himself! God has required from the beginning, a
portion of the increase from all His people. It is called a tithe [a tenth]
because it is 10%. That portion is meant to go to God's work and the
support of those doing it. In the Old Covenant it was meant to be duti-
fully observed and in the New Covenant it was upheld by Jesus [Matt.
23:23]. Now, if God owns the cattle on a thousand hills, why does He
need a tithe? Good question!

The tithe was ordained by God for our sakes, not for His! The giving
of the tithes and offerings was a major part of His law and required *faith*
to do it. He went so far as to demand of His people the first fruits of
their produce. That meant that after surviving the winter, being reduced
to the bottom of the food barrel, using the remainder of their grain for
seed and waiting till the first crops came up, they had to give the very
first of their income to God! In order to do that His people had to become free of the love of money. They could not obey that law unless
they first became unattached to their income. They had to literally cast
their lives and their concerns into God's hands. In many ways it was
like jumping off a cliff and hoping God's everlasting arms would be
there to catch them! It required living in a supernatural dimension.

THE SUPERNATURAL DIMENSION

They had to forsake everything that would give them worldly comfort and security [the income that was right in their hands] and look to
the dimension of God's Word and God's Promises. They had to have
trust that God's Word never fails and that He would surely care for

them. According to this word in Malachi 3:9-10, He would open the very windows of heaven and pour out a blessing too big to contain for those who obeyed.

In the New Covenant, the same principle exists except that Jesus opens the door wide to the spirit of the law. The spirit is that we can *"Give freely for freely it is given to you." Matt. 10:8.* No longer are we bound by the letter of the law that we must give, but we are given freedom to give without limit and without restraint. Jesus gives us wonderful promises such as Luke 6:38,

"Give and it shall be given unto you; good measure, pressed down, shaken together and running over, they will pour into your lap.

For by your standard of measure it will be measured to you in return."

As in the case with the Old Testament, stepping out to obey God's Word takes faith. Whether we are giving 10% of our paycheck to God's work or going above and beyond by freely and abundantly giving to others, in every case there is a point where we must let go of what we have in our hand to receive our needs being met by God Himself. We must enter a new dimension where God and His Word is so real that we can freely give away what we have in the total confidence that God will care for us. As you are in prayer while giving or waiting for God to act, there comes a point where you can almost, as it were, open a door by faith and step out into the real world where God will provide without fail even when it looks impossible! This gives us the freedom to obey the heart of this Commandment.

THE JOY OF OBEYING THIS COMMANDMENT

The heart of "Thou Shalt Not Steal" is that you no longer want everything for yourself but you want good for others as well. When you come upon a situation where you could take the best for yourself, God gives us a new heart that can be just as glad that someone else can have it. You take pleasure in their pleasure. Now with the freedom of Christ we can joyously give to others instead of taking from them. When we enter that new lifestyle, we are truly 'born again.' We are no longer living for ourselves but for others. With that change in heart attitude every one of the things mentioned in this lesson are easily and automatically fulfilled. Now we can gladly obey His word in Proverbs 19:17;

"He who is gracious to a poor man lends to the Lord,
And He will repay him for his good deed."

He who lends to someone who will not be able to repay it will be blessed by God Himself. That type of obedience is not possible unless you are first free from the love of money.

LESSON 18

THE NINTH COMMANDMENT

THOU SHALT NOT BEAR FALSE WITNESS
AGAINST THY NEIGHBOR

The Commandment consists of two parts. The first is that we should not bear any false witness, the second is we should not bear false witness against our neighbor. The former deals with *any* form of untruthfulness and is very broad in scope. The latter refers specifically to words we speak that will *hurt or injure others* in any way.

God is absolute truth and there is no untruth in Him. He is SEVERE truth. He is a bright, hot, searchlight turned upon a dark world. In Him there is no darkness at all. That means that there is nothing hidden in Him or hidden from Him.

"God is light and in Him there is no darkness at all.
If we say we have fellowship with Him and yet walk in the
darkness we lie and do not practice the truth." 1 John 1:5-6

"In Him was life, and the life was the light of men.
and the light shines in the darkness and the darkness did not
comprehend it." John 1:4-5

THE CHIEFTAIN
[A Story]

Upon a time there was a clan who had a wise and good chieftain. He ruled his people with justice and instructed them to be honest in all matters. Under his rule a man's integrity was never questioned. It was assumed that each man spoke with complete honesty. Because of this all dealings in the market were fair; deals could be concluded with a word and a handshake and disputes could be settled by simply inquiring into the matter. Many were the lawyers who turned sadly away from the town because there was no work for them! The general felicity resulting from the honesty of the people continued many years until the Chief was called away to settle a clan dispute. During his absence, the lawyers who were once sent away returned to set up their practices. They began by calling into question all that the Chieftain had taught and then began to convince the people that they all needed protection against  one another. Soon suspicion entered the hearts of the clansmen. They began to view one another differently, suspecting false motives and worrying that they weren't getting a fair deal. In a short time it became necessary for *everyone* to have a lawyer because they could trust no one. The legal profession was delighted. Once the mistrust was fully in motion it became a matter of course that the one with the most impressive lawyer could win their cases and thereby prosper greatly. Each one looked after their own interests and considered them foolish who were so unwise as to not be protected. This led to the final stage where if someone were unprotected, it was thought that they got what they deserved! If they were open to be swindled, it was *their* fault!

Had this occurred quickly it would have never taken root but because this took place over a period of time, the clan was unaware of how much they had lost. The once contented village was now a town under siege. Each man's home was barricaded against the reports and accusations of his fellow clansmen. It was thought to be the normal course of life now and eventually they forgot that they used to enjoy each other's company during the long winter nights.

The greatest battles were waged between two brothers who had acted as the Chief's lieutenants while he was away. Where they had once upheld the laws of the Chief, they had now so completely abandoned them that they fought one another with vicious lies. Lies bred lies and soon a day arrived when the brothers would face off against each other in court. Each hoped to completely ruin the other so that one of them would leave town. As the courtroom heated up and accusations flew about like rabid bats, suddenly there was a hush. All eyes were turned to one person who had entered. The Chief was in their midst. He had slipped quietly back to his village and now appeared in the middle of the courtroom. The reaction was palpable. His was unbelieving dismay at the behavior of his closest clansmen, theirs, horror.

With one motion he drew his great claymore and drove out the cringing lawyers, then he turned to his men. Their crimes were listed: they had forsaken the clan while the Chief was away, they had abandoned their post in rightly counselling the people, and they had led the clan into evil by their example. Their sentence was carried out and both of them were banished from the country. Their property was divided and given to the poorest tenant farmers.

And so peace was restored to the village and the clan. However, it was not without two lasting effects. The first was that those who loved the Chief were overwhelmed by relief because of his just government. They awoke as from a bad dream and made a solemn pledge that never again would they allow untruths and suspicion to pollute their view of their neighbors. These resumed the delightful fellowship that they once enjoyed. The second found that they could never quite trust anyone again. The poison had entered their bloodstream and continued to cause illness and death in them. Eventually these all moved away because they could no longer tolerate the Chief's demand for exact honesty in all dealings.

LIES DESTROY THE JOY OF SOCIETY

This story illustrates how any lies can infect society and cause mistrust on all sides. When that happens, there is a complete breakdown of society the way God intended it to be. What was meant to be pleasant is turned sour. The friendship and comradery which God made inherent to a community is lost and what remains, unfortunately, is clearly seen in many of our towns today. People are barricaded against the world outside because lies have turned salesmen into roving bandits and rampant backbiting has made the neighborhood a dreaded haven. When people bemoan missing a simpler country life, what they don't realize is that it's the neighborliness they miss the most. God did not make it that way. He wants to put the savor back into the community, starting with us! He calls them the 'salt of the earth' who are gentle, merciful peacemakers. So beginning with us, how do we achieve forthright honesty in our speech?

As mentioned, God's nature represents complete honesty. When

He shines His spotlight on our lives, it is truly shocking the number of ways we can speak untruthfully.

HALF TRUTHS

Half-truths are probably the most common area we stumble in. If you take the case of two children playing in a room, you might hear one of them complain that the other hit him. The way it's phrased you would get the clear picture that while one was innocently playing the other simply walked up and whacked him. In truth, they were both playing together, one said something nasty to the other, that one took the other child's toy, so on and so forth until it came to blows. When the little one ran and told his mother about being hit, he was actually bearing false witness by leaving out a large part of the story.

It is most unfortunate that what we see in small children reflects what we see in big adults. Sometimes it's unfathomable how little we learn as we grow up. Now as adults we continue the habit of telling half-truths to keep out of all types of trouble or to get others in trouble. A good example of this is our answer if a parent or a boss asks us if we did a certain chore. We answer yes, so we don't get in trouble, but we leave out the fact that we've only just begun or didn't complete the job. The ways we can lie in this area are too numerous to even list. Keep close track of your responses this week and you will be surprised at how many opportunities you have to tell less than the whole truth. You'll be even more shocked at how you answer.

BACKBITING

Humans have a strong tendency to want to make themselves look good. The easiest way to do that is to make others look worse. It is very difficult to actually be good, so instead we just make everyone else look bad. In the process we say a lot of unkind things about people and exaggerate a lot. That's why one of the rules that George Washington lived by was to 'never consider idle reports about others, they are likely to be false.' People love to tear others down and when we realize that, we don't pay much attention when we hear a wild report.

Consider carefully the words of Psalm 15:1-3;

"O Lord, who may abide in Thy tent? Who may dwell on
Thy holy hill?
He who walks with integrity and works righteousness, and speaks
truth in his heart.
He does not slander with his tongue, nor does evil to his neighbor,
nor takes up a reproach against his friend."

Amy Carmichael, the famous missionary to India in the early 1900s, made it a mandate within her compound that none should ever speak about someone else except in a good way. If there were conflicts, they were to be addressed to the individual only. In that way the "absent were safe" within their walls. She considered trust to be a sacred obligation, the very foundation upon which all relationship is built. Her rule strictly enforced brought peace and harmony to their village for one hundred years and it is still going on to this day!

If we were to follow her rule of silence unless it were edifying speech, how quiet would our week be? If we leave off speaking ill of others, how much conversation will be silenced? All this is directly in the realm of the Ninth Commandment. We are not to speak evil of others.

"He who covers a transgression seeks love,
But he who repeats a matter separates intimate friends."
Prov. 17:9

THE SEARCHLIGHT

Every man is right in his own eyes and so he justifies what he does and says. We might think that the little things we say aren't too bad compared to those around us. We see that criticizing one another is standard conversation in the world. Poor standard of measurement! If we compare ourselves to those around us, what will that do except to lull us into a false security that we're pretty good? Our standard is not the world. Our standard is Christ Himself. He is all truth and every falsehood is a major offense to Him. If we are covered with ashes  we can indeed take some comfort if we are surrounded with people covered with roofing tar. We can laugh at them while we're with them. We don't even have to worry about the ashes on us because the others are so much dirtier. But, if we are then led into a newly painted living room complete with brand new cream colored sofas and plush white carpet, suddenly we look very dirty.

So it is with God. While we look around us, it isn't difficult to imagine that we're pretty good. But when we come up to the Standard of Truth Himself, we will indeed say like the prophet "Woe is me, for I am a man of unclean lips." [Isaiah 6:5]

He is a searchlight and under His brilliant glare every flaw is detected. For those who desire fellowship with the Almighty, they must be prepared for extra close scrutiny. What will pass for the world will not pass for His children.

THE ACCUSER OF THE BRETHREN

The devil goes by several names, one of which is the 'father of lies'[John 8:44]. The other is the 'accuser of the brethren' [Rev. 12:10]. Both of these names pertain directly to us! He is the 'prince of the power of the air'[Eph. 2:2] and his influence is felt by all. Whenever false words are uttered and whenever accusing words are uttered, he is fulfilling his mission. He lives and breathes discord. He assists those he can use as instruments of disunity. That means whenever we personally fall to criticizing others, we are unwittingly in the service of the power of darkness. Think about that. With our critical words we fulfill his mission of 'lying' and 'accusing.' It's a fearful thought, isn't it? So we see that to speak evil is very, very easy. It's in the very air we breathe. If we do not want to fall into the category of devil's assistant we must work hard. We must go against an almost irresistible tide. Again, as before, the key is *almost*. God will help us if we seek Him night and day. As the apostle says, we '*have not yet resisted sin to the point of shedding blood in our fight against sin' Heb. 12:4*. God really does expect us to resort to drastic measures in our fight against all that would displease him.

117

Now we get to the sweet part of this commandment, that which is on the positive side. What do our lives to look like if we are obeying the commandment?

If the devil would have us lying about and accusing our neighbors and co-workers, God expects us to be doing exactly the opposite! God would have us to love and defend them. Think what that means in the practical sense. I will quote from Martin Luther's catechism here because he sums it up so perfectly:

"We must not say behind his back what we would not say to his face. We must not magnify his faults, nor impute evil motives to him, nor make his words and conduct look as bad as possible. The slanderer is worse than a thief and causes incalculable suffering and misery."

We must have "A charitable judgement of others. We should apologize for our neighbor and defend him when his character is unjustly assailed."

We must "Speak well of him whenever we can do so truthfully. We should speak of his virtues rather than his faults. If we cannot speak well of him, then, unless it is absolutely necessary, we had better not speak of him at all."

We should "Put the most charitable construction on all his actions. We should as far as possible make the best and not the worst of what our neighbor says and does. We should think and speak of him only in kindness."

Thus we see that the Law becomes a delight when we apply to it the overarching Law of Love. Not speaking ill of others becomes easy when we truly care about them! It is no chore to speak well of those we like. Jesus teaches us in Matthew 5:44-48;

"But I say to you love your enemies, and pray for those who
persecute you in order that you may be sons of your Father
who is in heaven;
For He causes His sun to rise on the evil and the good, and sends

118

rain on the righteous and the unrighteous.
For if you [only] love those who love you what reward have you?
Therefore you are to be perfect as your heavenly Father is perfect."

LOVE THY ENEMY, ARE YOU KIDDING?

Of course the next question is how do we love those who are mean to us? It is not an easy thing to be nice to someone who is hurting you in some way. The key to that is found in the verse - *"pray for those who persecute you."* You must start with an act of shear obedience. You will not want to do it, but you must. As you begin to pray for that person, ask God to make you sincere. As you continue, you will find a supernatural softening taking place in your soul. It will start with God beginning to cool your offense and then as you pray on, you will start to think of him or her as a person. If you continue still, you will be enabled to actually begin  to love them. It may start in the form of pity but it will grow from there. One thing you will learn is that it's impossible to hate someone you're praying for. As you linger in the presence of God all ungodly attitudes will dissolve!

So the secret of obedience lies in seeking the presence of God. Psalm 31:20 says,

> *"Thou dost hide them in the secret place of Thy presence from the conspiracies of man*
> *Thou dost keep them secretly in a shelter from the strife of tongues."*

It is necessary for us to remember that this earnest seeking is not optional for God's people. He requires it of us. Let me end with this good promise from Proverbs 3:3-4,

> *"Do not let kindness and truth leave you. Bind them on around your neck.*
> *Write them on the tablet of your heart.*
> *So you will find favor and good repute in the sight of God and man."*

119

LESSON 19

THE TENTH COMMANDMENT

THOU SHALT NOT COVET

GOD'S WORD TO THE CHURCH

Though there are many sins plaguing the church today perhaps the most rampant of all is the breech of the commandment concerning covetousness. It has infected the church like a cancer and very few are untouched by its influence. There is a reason for that. We are all too ready and willing to be enticed by worldly cravings and the promise that God will fulfill all the desires of our heart, whether godly or otherwise. So we listen readily to any and all who would promise us riches, dreams and personal fulfillment - if only we give to their particular ministry!

What we see in the Bible, however, stands in bold contrast to the claims of worldly wealth. In fact Jesus warns us that it is a great snare to our souls, something to be on constant guard against. It is the enemy of all true progress in a Godly direction. Let us consider an interesting example found in the book of 1 Samuel chapter 15.

CATTLE, WHAT CATTLE?

At this time God had just established Israel's first king at their request. Through the prophet Samuel, God had anointed Saul to be ruler over all the tribes. His first commission as king was to bring God's just punishment on the Amalekites who practiced vile pagan sacrifices and had persecuted the Israelites on their journey from Egypt. He was strictly instructed by God not to touch any of the spoil. None was to be taken because it was defiled in the sight of God. Saul bravely went about the Lord's business and did all that was asked of him....to a point. While he was in the midst of the city he saw the choice spoils that lay about him on all sides and his heart was drawn to them. He was neither able to destroy them nor leave them behind.

But Saul spared "the best of the sheep, the oxen, the fatlings, the lambs and all that was good, and was not willing to destroy them utterly;"

But *"everything despised and worthless, that they utterly destroyed." 1Sam. 15:9*

The result was, he took the good with him. Then the word of the Lord came to Samuel saying *"I regret that I have made Saul king, for he has turned back from following Me."* The prophet then goes to Saul to confront him about his misdeeds. Saul, flushed with his victory joyously tells him how he has accomplished God's work. Samuel then asks a very pointed question saying, *"What then is this bleating of sheep in my ears and the lowing of oxen which I hear?"* Saul's answer serves as a model for all who follow in his steps. He immediately shifts gears and explains to Samuel that he has brought the animals to sacrifice to the Lord! He puts the best possible face on what he has done all the while trying desperately to escape the burning eyes of the man of God. Samuel will not be put off and says *"The Lord sent you on a mission." "Why then did you not obey*  the voice of the Lord, but rushed upon the spoil and did what was evil in the sight of the Lord?"* Saul argues more about the proposed godly use of the spoils, but Samuel concludes with these words,

"Has the Lord as much delight in burnt offerings and sacrifices as in obeying the voice of the Lord?

Behold to obey is better than sacrifice and to heed than the fat of rams.

For rebellion is as the sin of divination and insubordination is as iniquity and idolatry.

Because you have rejected the word of the Lord, He has also rejected you from being king." 1Sam. 15

He then said God's Spirit and the kingdom would be removed from him and given to a better man.

THIS SPEAKS TO THE CHURCH TODAY

This story has many frightful consequences to us in the Western Church, for many of our leaders have followed Saul's leadership rather than King David's [who was the Godly king who came after him]. Beginning on a mission to serve God they are enticed by the spoils and 'fall upon them.' Spoils have never been easier to fall upon or harder to avoid. A single 'prophetic word' proclaiming God's blessing on those who give to their ministry can yield thousands or millions of dollars to those leaders who might have initially been sincere. But as covetousness runs rampant in their hearts, they rush headlong into the error of Balaam, who 'prophesied' for pay. [2 Peter 2:15]

The next step is to justify it as Saul did. He said that the riches were to be 'used for God's work.' How familiar does that sound? No expense is spared for lavish worldly edifices. No perks are too shameful for them. The money heaped upon them by the unsuspecting is considered their due! The spoils are used as a sign that God is blessing them!

Foolish preachers. But their shame is not finished yet, for the next thing is to make their followers the same as they are. So the enticement of greed, avarice, worldly riches and the fulfillment of all the heart's desires is stock in trade for their 'sermons.' Anything goes as long as you put the name of God on it. His Holy Name becomes the passport to the land of all corruption. Teaching that God's Word can be used to obtain all your covetous desires, it's no wonder that their churches are  filled to overflowing! Meanwhile a short distance away is a tiny church where the minister faithfully represents Jesus' teaching. And what makes his church so small? Jesus taught His followers to live a life of self denial! He instructed them that true life cannot be found in any earthly things, that the greatest and only joy can only be obtained by casting your own desires away to serve Him and others. No wonder he has so few attending! How could that compete with the new gospel where God's will is that He would be the source of every earthly thing you ever desired? It is not hard to imagine which church Jesus would be comfortable attending. Unfortunately this greed based, comfortable western gospel is no longer contained to the west but has gained great ground all over the world.

Here's what Jesus has to say concerning these things:

*"Do not lay up for yourselves treasures upon earth where moth and
rust destroy and where thieves break in and steal,
But lay up for yourselves treasures in heaven, where neither moth
nor rust destroys and where thieves do not break in and steal."
Matthew 6:19-20
"No one can serve two masters; for either he will hate the one and
love the other, or he will hold to one and despise the other.
You cannot serve God and mammon [money]. Matt.6:24*

*"And the one on whom seed was sown among the thorns, this is the
man who hears the word and the worry of the world and the
deceitfulness of riches choke the word and it becomes
unfruitful." Matt. 13:22.*

With just these few passages we can see much of what is taught
today in the name of Jesus is far from Jesus' own teaching. This should
actually make us afraid. He said *"If anyone wishes to come after Me,
let him deny himself, and take up his cross and follow Me."* This is in
direct reference to worldly wealth, for the next lines are *"For what will
a man be profited if he gains the whole world and forfeits his soul?"*
Matt. 16:24-26

A SINGLE EYE

Jesus teaches us that we must have a 'single eye' in following Him.
What He means by that is that we must have a single focus. Our eyes
must be directly on Him and must not stray to the left or right. If they
do we may be immediately drawn to some alluring attraction that will
threaten our soul by distracting us from the path of life. I love to think
about Jesus 'setting His face like flint for Jerusalem.' Nothing was going to distract Him from accomplishing His Father's will. And He had
to be determined because we can be sure that His own human flesh did
not desire to do the thing before Him. His flesh recoiled at the thought
of being nailed to a cross the same as ours would. Now we must also

follow in our Beloved Master's footsteps and set *our* faces like flint for the *New Jerusalem*. We must be doggedly determined to obey Him by keeping our eyes off those things that would pollute our souls with covetousness. Not easy to do in a society that's whole economic and spiritual foundation lies in enticing people to obtain worldly goods by every means possible. From morning to night we are bombarded with advertisements which sole purpose is to stimulate covetousness in us! For us it is imperative that we remember Jesus' admonition *"For where your treasure is there will your heart be also." Matt. 6:21*

FALSE PROPHETS

If anyone teaches something contrary to the Lord's own teaching, do not listen no matter how popular the speaker is or how acclaimed. Jesus said *"the sheep follow him because they know his voice, and a stranger they simply will not follow, but will flee from him, because they do not know the voice of strangers."* We follow the Master, and we simply will not go after others. Where false teachers gain so much ground among ordinary and good-hearted believers is that many or even most average Christians have not read the Bible for themselves. The Word is our shield and if we have not picked it up, we will be defense-less against those who promote covetousness 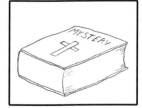 within the church as though it were a godly trait, then proceed to bilk the unsuspecting and leave town bragging of their success. Interestingly, in this same passage, Jesus is specifically referring to the strangers as those who come as thieves and robbers. They always come in the appearance of shepherds of the flock. For those who have not taken up their full defense yet by reading through the entire Bible for themselves, here is the clear teaching of scripture concerning the modern gospel of worldly wealth;

"Men of depraved mind and deprived of the truth, who suppose
that godliness is a means of gain."
"For we have brought nothing into the world and we cannot take
anything out of it either.
And if we have food and clothing with these we shall be content.
But those who want to get rich fall into temptation and a snare
and many foolish and harmful desires which plunge men into

ruin and destruction.

*For the love of money is a root of all sorts of evil, and some by
longing for it have wandered away from the faith and pierced
themselves with many a pang.*

*But flee from these things you man of God and pursue
righteousness, godliness, faith, love, perseverance and
gentleness." 1 Tim: 6:5-11*

This is what the apostle Peter has to say on the same matter;

*These teachers have "eyes full of adultery and that never cease
from sin, enticing unstable souls, having a heart trained in
greed, accursed children."*

*"These are springs without water and mists driven by a storm for
whom the black darkness has been reserved.*

*For speaking out arrogant words of vanity they entice by fleshly
desires, by sensuality those who barely escape from the ones
who live in error.*

*Promising freedom while they themselves are slaves of
corruption." 2 Peter 2*

FALSE PROPHETS DON'T KNOW IT

Again, we must remember that no one who is a false teacher realizes that fact at the time. When God removes all discernment no one
can see their error. Because of that, they speak with great confidence
and courage, fully assured that God is smiling with His approval. Jesus'
words in Matthew 7:21-23 are very sobering. He says,

*"Many will say to Me on that day, 'Lord, Lord did we not
prophesy in Your name, and cast out demons and in Your name
perform many miracles?*

*And then I will declare to them, 'I never knew you; depart from
Me you who practice lawlessness."*

These ministers, preachers, teachers and prophets mentioned here
had absolutely no idea that they were not the apple of God's eye! And
so it is today. And why were they cast out? For lawlessness. And what
law is most frequently broken by them? The law against covetousness
and greed. If the law of God is neglected, every type of sin and error

can creep into the church undetected. That is why we ourselves must read and study to know what's approved. We do not want to be swept away with the false teachers and the multitudes of those who follow.

HIS CHILDREN'S LIFESTYLE

God has given us His word and He expects us to use it. It's imperative that we personally pick it up and use it to keep on the straight path. All these enticing teachings sound good and plausible until we pull out the gospel and read Jesus' own words. His words are the compass, that's why we stress reading the Bible for yourself. Don't take our word for it or anybody else's. Study and ask the Holy Spirit to guide you into all truth. And be careful to read a time-tested translation of the Bible [KJV, NKJV, NASB to name a few]. Some new hip versions have actually been altered to fit these vain teachings.

Now we come to actually working out the commandment in our daily lives. As with the other commandments all is naturally and completely fulfilled by the single ingredient of God's love. Here are some of the things we can be covetous of and how the fulfillment of the law changes our response to them.

THY NEIGHBOR'S WIFE

We can be covetous of our friend's wife or husband. They could be attractive and funny and attentive to us. They could make us feel as though we're still desirable to someone instead of simply taken

for granted by our current spouse. These are powerful stimulants. Indeed, so powerful that none could resist but by the intervening grace of God. The strong grip of attraction is evidenced by the prolific abundance of extramarital affairs and divorces, both outside and within the church.

Now as children of God, our response must be twofold. The first is that we beg Him for the strength to resist temptation. That in itself requires a miracle born of ardent and fearful prayer. Second is the duty we owe our friends to not alienate their spouses from them. While we flirt or delight in someone else's company, we are both playing with true spiritual death and committing a crime against their own spouses by drawing away their lawful attention to their legal mates. That may not seem like a big deal at the time because, of course, the first and last rationale is that 'my spouse doesn't pay any attention to me.' We use this to justify our actions and divert the blame to the innocent party! But God knows the spouse who is being alienated from their husband or wife, and He is on their side! He doesn't take your side because you feel so neglected. He is on the side of the Law. So, someone who has not actually committed the sin of adultery and yet causes the spouse of someone else to be turned toward himself is guilty of breaking this Commandment. This is a far reaching statement and requires a constant guard of our hearts and tongues!

ANYTHING THAT BELONGS TO YOUR NEIGHBOR

Another meaning for covetous is to be envious. We can be envious of many things that belong to someone else and it can burn a hole into our hearts. We can be envious of their beautiful new home, or their expensive sports car. We can be envious of their high paying job, or we can envy their leisure. They seem to be able to go away on vacations all the time! These things can eat at us and if left unchecked produce great misery in ourselves. The net result is that they make us discontented with what we have. And so all the good we have is lost by a desire for the good we don't have. So covetousness poisons our soul and prevents us from enjoying life. Paul speaks wonderfully to this point in Philippians 4,

"For I have learned to be content in whatever circumstances I am.
I know how to get along with humble means and also how to live
with prosperity;
In any and every circumstance I have learned the secret of being
filled and going hungry,
Both of having abundance and suffering need.
I can do all things through Christ who strengthens me."
Isn't it interesting that the oft quoted verse *" I can do all things throught*

Christ who strengthens me." is actually refering to being content with nothing?

JESUS WALKED

Our wonderful freedom in Christ is that we are unconcerned with the passing pleasures of this life! What does it matter to us if we spend our life in toil when we have an eternity of delight before us. What difference does it make if our neighbor or friend lives in a grand house? You can be sure they are no happier for it! And we follow in the footsteps of our Beloved who had no home at all! Should it be that we live in splendor while we claim to be followers of a poor, righteous carpenter? Should that be our goal? Again we see the great disparity between the modern teaching and the lifestyle of Christ. He showed that the one who could lay aside all to follow Him was the richest of all! And who cares what kind of car you drive? If you follow the crowd instead of the Savior, you'll find yourself behind the wheel of a fancy four wheel drive. How many less fortunate people are you causing to stumble by your ostentatious display of 'abundant life?' So you break the commandment and you also cause others to break it. Not a very enviable position if you ask me! Jesus walked.

Our freedom is the Cross of Christ. We, like Paul, can learn to be content in whatever circumstances we are in. *"Not even when you have abundance does life consist of these things" Luke 12:15.* We have died and our life is hidden in Christ. When He is revealed, we also will be revealed with Him in glory [Col. 3:3, 4].

LESSON 20

OUR FREEDOM IN CHRIST

We come now to the joyous freedom that we have in Christ. It is not freedom as the world views it, but it is a freedom that is vastly superior and completely out of reach to any but Jesus' followers.

I once did some work in a little town called Freedom. Though I don't know what the town was like when it was founded, I could see that the particular type of freedom enjoyed by the town's people now was based on their freedom to do whatever they wanted. The town was situated in a remote northern area which gave the locals a certain confidence that they would not have the interference of the law in their pursuits. That gave them the liberty to engage in all types of behavior that might otherwise be restricted. This is the freedom which the carnal or earthly-minded person considers the greatest of all - freedom to do what ever they want, whenever they want. Essentially it is the freedom to behave badly without restraint. The devil, when God allows, enjoys this type of freedom.

OUR FREEDOM TO BE GOOD - THE NARROW GATE

But there is another meaning for the word freedom and it is the meaning Jesus refers to when He says in John 8:31,
"If you abide in My word, then you are truly disciples of Mine;
And you shall know the truth and the truth shall make you free."
This freedom is not based upon having no restrictions, but on the freedom to do what is right! That's a true freedom because no one can do things which are difficult and require patience and self control without God's help. We can't and don't want to stop engaging in the liberty to have our own way. The fact is we are slaves to sin. Jesus said,
"Truly, truly I say to you, everyone who commits sin is a slave to
sin. And the slave does not remain in the house forever." John 8:34
So, Jesus introduces a new freedom, which is the freedom to follow Him in obedience. This is the narrow gate. He says in John 8:36,
"If therefore the Son shall make you free, you are free indeed."
Now we have the glorious ability to actually walk along side Jesus to wherever He leads.

OUR FREEDOM IS THE CROSS

"If anyone wishes to come after Me, let him deny himself,
and take up his cross daily and follow Me." Luke 9: 23

With these words Jesus turned our world upside down. Rather than the greatest good being the obtaining of all our hearts desires and all our creature comforts, He tells us that our goal is to pick up our cross daily to follow Him! And what does it mean to pick up the cross? What did it mean to Jesus?

Jesus' example shows us clearly what it means. His life demonstrated two different aspects of bearing the cross. The first was literally picking it up. He laid aside every natural impulse to save His own life and avoid unnecessary pain in order to give Himself up to a brutal and torturous death. Jesus did not have to do that. It would not have personally cost Him anything to simply leave us in the state we were in. He could have walked away at any time. Like any other ruler, He had the option of sacrificing us or saving our lives.

A KING'S RANSOM
[A Story]

In a far off land lived a great King, legitimate son to the Emperor. His domain extended far and wide and was notable for the peacefulness of its citizens. The King's remarkable wisdom and justice caused good will and harmony to prevail throughout his realm.

After a time, some of his more difficult subjects looked about and saw another land a good way off in the distance that looked desirable to them. It seemed fertile and promising and better than the land they now occupied, but it lay just outside the borders of the empire. After some deliberation, they decided to set out in spite of the boundary.

The King dispatched several of his most trusted aids to warn them of the danger of venturing out of his domain. A cruel warlord occupied the lands just outside the kingdom, who ruled by force and terror. But the unruly subjects abused the messengers and told them to get out of the way. They exclaimed "We can see for ourselves that it is a prosperous land, and we won't be stopped." They said this because lately they had begun to suspect that the King was simply withholding the best land from them to use for himself. Those emissaries that refused to get out of the way they actually killed.

Once they reached the new land the greedy eyes of the Warlord lit up with an evil green fire. Now he finally had a means of bringing down his hated enemy, the King. He would use these willful wanderers as his bargaining chip. Immediately, he sent off a message to the king stating his intent to slay every man, woman and child that had ventured into his territory. They would be slaughtered without mercy. He kept the people themselves unaware of the danger though because he did not want to set off any alarm. If panic ensued some of them might escape! So the doomed citizens were kept blissfully uninformed of their deadly situation.

Knowing the unalterable justice of the King, the Warlord was aware that he was well within his rights to kill them all. The subjects had willfully turned away. The King would not be able to *legally* fight him either in a court or battlefield. He would have to strike a bargain!

The good King slowly turned away from the Warlord's ambassadors after he had read the message. He knew there was only one thing that would satisfy his enemy's quest for blood. There was only one way that he could bring the release of his people legally. He would make the Warlord an offer he couldn't refuse. He would give himself in exchange for them!

The Warlord howled with delight as the day of doom and justice arrived and the great, noble King voluntarily surrendered himself into his enemy's camp. Because of his extreme contempt, the Warlord was not content to simply kill the King, he would first subject him to ridicule and humiliation! So he paraded him through the streets after shaving his head and dressing him in a jester's suit. To add to the insult, the king's own rebellious subjects turned out to join the proceedings! They entered in with the rest, jeering their King, mocking him and saying "You thought you were so high and mighty, look at you now!"

When the Warlord was content that the King was sufficiently humiliated, he next subjected him to various tortures. His was to be no quick death! He whipped and beat him mercilessly while taunting and spitting in his face. Finally he hung his body on the wall of his city so everyone could see his great triumph. And slowly the King died.

At the moment of his death the contract was fulfilled. He had com-

pleted the terms in full and now the Warlord would have to release the Emperor's subjects. It couldn't be broken, they were legally free to go.

But the Warlord still had one more card to play. Though he knew he must let them go legally, what was to stop him from simply hiding that knowledge from them? He had already concealed his plan to kill them, what could be easier than neglecting to mention they were now free? As many as could be kept ignorant of their position would still remain his property to do with as he pleased! And so the Warlord began to use his lever of their ignorance to his best advantage.

Meanwhile, the King's trusted servants had been instructed in what to do. The King knew full well what could be expected from his enemy, and so had prepared his men to go forth into the enemy's territory immediately after his death to inform his subjects that they were now free. And go they did. Frequent parties went out into all parts of the land to tell them the good news that they were able to return to their home.

Amazingly, their reception was mixed. In some cases rather than being greeted with cheers, they became targets of rotten fruit thrown at them! Many of the rebellious subjects had grown content in their new environment. They had accepted the cruelty and strife that prevailed under the Warlord's rule as a normal part of living. There was not a trace of memory of the delightful peace that they once had under the King. It was also impossible to convince them of the imminent danger they were in. For those there was little hope. Being content under the cruelty of the Warlord and being ignorant of their danger, these actually led the opposition to the King's men! The Warlord's designs had not changed and his greatest victory over the King would be to kill his subjects even after he sacrificed his life for them! His ultimate triumph would be for the king to die in vain!

Others were distressed over leaving the King's domain and were sorry in many ways that they had rebelled. Their time under the Warlord had taken its toll and they were tired of his ways. These received the ambassadors with gladness. When they heard the story of their perilous position and all the king had done for them, they were astonished. They had neither known about the Warlord's decree to execute them nor of the King's willing sacrifice to purchase their freedom. Some left right away for the safety of home and lived in a state of constant gratitude towards the memory of their King who had made it possible for them to escape. Others, from that moment on didn't cease to join the rest in proclaiming the truth of the matter to all those around them. Their love for the King knew no bounds. Many willingly faced fierce opposition in the hope that some would listen. No sacrifice was too great and no difficulty too hard in their work of telling others. Hadn't their Lord and King given himself up freely for them? Should they do less? In the end the Warlord did manage to deceive many of the King's people right to the last. These he devoured with the sword as his last act of vengeance to the King. But, the story did not end there.

The Great Emperor, father of the King visited the land again. When he heard the events he proceeded immediately to execute vengeance on the murderer of his son. The Warlord was utterly defeated and his lands confiscated. The choicest of the regions were then handed over to those of his subjects who had willingly joined in, proclaiming the truth and rescuing all they could. Though grateful, these subjects could hardly accept the Emperor's gracious offer. After all wasn't it their own rebelliousness that had caused all the trouble? Nevertheless, the

Emperor called them faithful servants and insisted on their receiving his reward. And so the land regained its peace and justice, and the well-being of the people exceeded even what it had been before.

OUR SELFLESS KING

Our blessed King actually did that for us! There was nothing to bind Him to it. He could have obliterated us. Or He could have abandoned us to our rightful fate. But, He didn't! He really did sacrifice Himself on our behalf so that we could be released from a cruel enemy - an enemy which for the most part we don't even know about!

Let's review why Jesus had to die for us to be set free. God gave His children a command and told them they would die if they disobeyed it. His children didn't listen and did exactly what He forbade them to do. If God simply forgave them and there was no punishment it would mean His word meant nothing. It would mean in the future they could break His laws and get away with it. The 10 Commandments would be turned into the 10 Suggestions. They would become perpetual offenders. This is the essence of why children are so disobedient today. Their parents tell them not to do something or they will be punished. They do exactly what they are told not to do and instead of being punished they are simply forgiven. Their behavior is excused because they don't know any better. The forgiveness is good and no parent stops loving their children because they disobey, but by not following through with a punishment they teach their children they can disobey without any consequence. For their word to be respected in the future they had to carry out the punishment. In the same way we [mankind] had to be punished in order to uphold God's word. And this is where the wisdom and love of God is so wonderful... Jesus Himself offered to take our place at the execution.

So the first part of Jesus' own example was literally laying down His life for us. He faced the complete death of His honor by allowing himself to be mocked and humiliated. If you think back to the last time someone made fun of you, you can remember how it burned and stung. Here He was, the King, and He was being scorned by subjects which He could have wiped out with a single word! Then He was subjected to cruel tortures and finally hung up on a cross to endure a slow agonizing death. All this He did for the ungrateful subjects whose own willful rebellion had put them in danger of death!

But that was not all, that was just one costly decision. What led up to it was the *second* aspect of picking up of the cross. Just as He instructed us to deny ourselves and take up our cross daily, so He demonstrated it for us as an example. Jesus' earthly life from beginning to end was one complete cross. What the cross means in daily life is as follows.

OUR OWN AGENDA

Each of us has our own will and our own desires. From the time we get up until we turn out the light before bed, each one of us has our own agenda. That agenda usually or always has our own best good and desires at the bottom of it. When that agenda is interrupted, whether it's a phone call while we're watching TV or your wife or mother asking you to do the dishes, the reaction is predictable. Our temper flares or we whine or we put it off or we just make up an excuse or don't do it. That is the natural human reaction. It comes with the package of being born here. Its root is complete selfishness. We're doing something we like and someone is interfering with it. When Jesus said we were slaves

Would you do the dishes, honey?

of sin, that's what He meant. Our selfishness is not something we want to give up and our dealings with those around us flow from that selfish mindset. When it comes to those we live with, it can get very ugly.

Jesus demonstrated a radical break from human nature. He willingly gave up His own agenda in order to follow His Father's wishes! It is one thing to do that with some big project that you can work yourself up to doing and it is completely another matter when you are interrupted on a moment by moment basis. That is what it means by dying daily and taking up your cross daily. To be able to be interrupted, to be able to have your agenda changed in order to accommodate someone else's desires is the Divine Nature. Jesus constantly prayed 'not My will Father but Your will be done.' This was not just before going to His death, this was His lifestyle. It was because of the daily surrendering of His own will to God that He was able to walk one day at a time right up to the point of lying down on rough, crossed timbers. This is the amazing Master that we want to serve.

LOVE AND SELFISHNESS CANCEL EACH OTHER

So now because of the grace of God and the outpouring of His Holy Spirit we are able to walk beside that Master. As He picked up His cross daily so we can and must pick up our cross as well. We can allow Him to crucify our own natural tendencies, our own selfish desires, our own personal comfort in order that we might become true children of His Father. That crucifying process is the one absolute necessity for actually entering into the love which fulfills the heart of the Law. Again, this is the narrow gate which few ever find. Love and selfishness are opposites. Where there is selfishness no love can dwell. So we can attend church all we want and we can talk the talk of one who's saved, but the measure of true Christ-likeness is in how we love. In order to love as He loves, the self, our self, must be put to death. How does that look in real life?

LOVING GOD

In our love for God it means real obedience. Remember, Jesus said He and His Father would make their home only with those who *obeyed* Him. Real obedience means living for God. He must become our first and last concern of the day and pleasing Him must be the driving force of our daily life. We must be willing to make Him the top priority. When God is truly first in our life it means we are waiting for Him to bring us assignments and tasks. Instead of determining to get our agenda done each day, we pray in the morning that God would accomplish His purposes through us that day. We then look for His divine appointments. Instead of being wrapped up in our pursuits we remember that nothing we do that day matters at all except what is done for Him. All our other work and pursuits are simply wood, hay and stubble built on a fine golden foundation. We must actually be anticipating Him to interrupt us!

The other part of our death to self in regard to loving God is that we put off our own pleasure and comforts to spend time with Him. It is a small and pleasant sacrifice to spend time with the River of Delights, and yet God still blesses it as though it were really a sacrifice! I'm reminded of George Whitefield who preached to crowds of 30-50,000 throughout England and America before there even was a United States. Why did God bless his efforts so mightily? In his early days Mr. Whitefield made it his practice to study and pray for eight hours every day before he went out to minister! He would then often preach, teach and counsel for all that remained of the day and frequently half the night! His only complaint was he often wished there were more hours in the day. Any time you set apart to be with God, He will bless.

LOVING OUR NEIGHBOR

Denying ourselves in regard to those around us means think-ing of them rather than ourselves. This is a monumental task which requires daily and hourly crucifixion. It means when a telemarketer calls in the middle of supper, remembering that it is a *person*. They are people just like you that have families and bills and needs of their own. They aren't humanoids. The telemarketer you were just rude to now has to call 500 more people just like you! If they don't they can't make their car payment or their rent. And how do you know that their mother hasn't recently been admitted to the hospital with terminal cancer? Every person on earth has trials and troubles, many worse than yours! What if that is the person that God *specifically sent* to you for a kind word?

It means next time you're just settling in to watch a game and are called upon to do something for somebody, you are willing to do it, *and* you do it without so much as exhaling loudly! Philippians 2: 14-16 says,

"Do all things without grumbling or disputing, that you may prove
yourself to be blameless and innocent children of God above
reproach in the midst of a crooked and perverse generation,
Among whom you appear as lights in the world,
holding fast to the word of life."

That is truly picking up your cross and God is pleased to call you his son or daughter! We always think in such grand terms, but it's the smallest things that really show what's in our hearts.

It means when you're called upon to do something extra at work for no extra pay, you simply do it. And you do it with a pleasant attitude with the only reward being that you're helping someone. These are all tiny examples of taking up the cross but these will tell the world that you are a follower of Jesus!

BEAR THE INSULT

Another way to pick up your cross daily is bearing criticism without reacting. Each of us is criticized many times throughout the day either by our spouse, our siblings, our children, our friends, our co-workers, or our boss. Most people have a very hard time with criticism. It cuts them to the quick and makes them feel useless and unappreciated. It is most frequently dispensed by those closest to us because they feel they have the liberty to do so. That makes it worse because these are the people we really care about. Taking up Jesus' cross is the only way to have peace within the home or workplace. It means simply bearing the insult. Let's say that again - it means simply bearing the insult. Nothing on earth can be harder than doing this one thing. It requires

true death to self and that is the essence of the cross. And yet it is demanded of us. Jesus again, led by example. Being falsely accused by the religious leaders and by His own people, 'Jesus opened not His mouth.' He did not speak in His own defence. He did not rail against the injustice that was taking place. He was quiet. There never was a more innocent person than He and no one who could have more loudly protested His innocence. He trusted Himself into the Father's hands.

It says in Hebrews 12:2,

"Fixing our eyes on Jesus, the Author and perfecter of faith,
who for the joy set before Him endured the cross,
Despising the shame, and has sat down
at the right hand of the throne of God."

Here again our most Blessed Savior demonstrated the type of life He desires to see in those who come after Him. He endured with complete quietness of spirit the most cruel and bitter words that could have been thrown against Him. He expects no less of us.

This example also typifies another type of criticism we will face if we become a true disciple of Christ - we will be persecuted. That persecution may be in the form of cruel jokes, or unfair treatment or it could be literal bodily harm. From the smallest criticism to the greatest physical torture our God wants us to endure without retaliation. Consider the rest of this passage in Hebrews 12,

"For consider Him who endured such hostility by sinners
against Himself, so that you may not grow weary and lose heart.
You have not yet resisted to the point of shedding blood in your
striving against sin." Heb. 12:3-4

THE SECRET POWER OF GOD

The secret to doing this is found in the same scripture. It says 'for the joy set before Him' He endured the cross. God has established a failproof mechanism in the universe, it is one of those laws of God. If anyone silently endures mistreatment, God will Himself both turn the ultimate outcome to that person's good and also miraculously strengthen them during the difficultly. It says in the 31st Psalm,

"How great is Thy goodness which Thou hast stored up for
those who fear Thee,
Which Thou hast wrought for those who take refuge in Thee.
Thou dost hide them in the secret place of Thy presence from
the conspiracies of man.
Thou dost keep them secretly in a shelter from the strife
of tongues." Psalm 31:19-20

It is truly a marvel to see how God comes to our aid when we, following His example, are silent before our accusers. A supernatural peace comes over us and we know we have His approval. That peace is the 'secret place' that David is referring to. It is real, it fills us and it even brings us joy! This is something that cannot ever be experienced until we actually obey Jesus' command to pick up our cross. Try it yourself.

STAND UP FOR YOURSELF?

Abandon the council of the world which demands that we "stand up for ourselves," and argues 'If you don't stand up for your rights no one else will" That is completely untrue! If we *don't* stand up for ourselves, *God* will stand up for us! Go completely against the grain of every self-assertiveness seminar and follow Jesus. Be silent. You will be amazed by what happens. God will suddenly become your defender because He will be on your side! This wonderful principle will work whether you simply don't react next time a family member criticizes you or you bear up under persecution. God will hide you in the shelter of His presence from the strife of tongues.

Following Jesus in real obedience to picking up the cross is the surprising door to radiant life. It is contrary to all teaching about putting yourself first. As we lay down our life we find we gain it!

LESSON 21

TAKING UP OUR CROSS DAILY

HOW MUCH IS YOUR SOUL WORTH?

So far we have covered two areas of picking up our own cross to follow Jesus. The first was following Him in spite of persecution. This could be anything from open confrontation to pressure from those around us not to become fanatical. Most often it is the people closest to us that become the means of hindering our forward progress in the things of God. It will be family members and friends who will become the most vocal in their opposition to your new radical step of following Christ. I have witnessed over the years many occasions where a young person is engaged in a lifestyle of complete corruption - parties, drugs, drunkenness, immorality, etc. The parents are concerned but do not go so far as to intervene. They rationalize that "It's just a phase," and "We were the same when we were young." But, if a new element is introduced and the young person is led into a living relationship with God, suddenly the parents take notice. Immediately they are very much involved with the 'safety' of their child. Where it would have been fine to stay out all night with a girlfriend or boyfriend, now it is completely unacceptable to go to a prayer meeting! The parent's concern about their child becoming a fanatic is overwhelming.

The prince of the power of the air will do anything to stop you from becoming a child of God. But if you do become a child of God, he will do anything to hinder you from moving on. You must be prepared to fight for your soul! If you decide to follow Christ with your whole heart, you will get opposition from the most unexpected sources. Friends who never cared one bit about you will now be overly protective, trying to make it seem as if it were for your own good to abandon your new love for God. Be on guard and don't be put off. It costs something to follow our loving Savior. In many Islamic nations the cost of following Jesus is literally the loss of your family and in many cases the loss of your life. Yet young people still make the commitment. Why? Because their eternal soul is worth the price! How much is your soul worth?

THE SERVANT OF ALL

The second area we covered was picking up our cross in relation to other people. This involves the daily practice of laying aside our own concerns and pleasures for sake of others. Jesus again turned the world upside down when He gave us His words *"The greatest among you will be the servant of all" Mark 10:43-45*. With these words He demonstrated our need to enter into a servant mentality. A servant is always concerned with pleasing the master. That is what they do. It is their job. If their master tells them to take care of some guests of his, they do so without any questions. The servant doesn't ask whether the guests are worthy of his care, nor does he suggest that he could be better employed elsewhere. He simply does his duty to his master.

In the same way, if we would become great in the Kingdom of God the road lies in the path of servanthood. Whoever God brings to you during the day is the one He wants you to take care of. No questions, just service. Some may seem unworthy of the attention, but who are we to decide what the Master would have us do?

To have the heart of a servant prepares us perfectly to do His will, fulfilling the spirit of the law, not just the letter. We can then serve others with a good attitude, not in a grudging way. I actually would like to go even beyond the concept of being a servant and encourage us to think in terms of being His slaves. As a servant we might consider ourselves to have some rights as part of the household,  but as slaves we do not even consider having any rights at all. A servant will do well and be approved by God, but a slave will find himself or herself great in the Kingdom of God. Remember, it is he who is the greatest servant who is the closest to following the Great Servant. As with the situation of bearing with people's criticism we will find servanthood and even more, slavehood, to be rewarded in the same way. The God of all peace will come to you and make His home with you and you will have a supernatural comfort that no one else can even comprehend. Servanthood - the surprising door to a radiant life!

THE CROSS IS THE ATTRACTION

That supernatural peace which God grants to His beloved is what prompted the missionary Amy Carmichael to claim that 'the cross is the attraction.' What she meant by this was that the very real sense of God's approval and His intimate fellowship so outweighed the pleasures of the world that picking up the cross of Christ becomes the most attractive thing we can do. She made it a stipulation that no one could join the ranks of her mission outpost unless they clearly understood this principle. They had to do as Paul did;

"Count all things as loss in view of the surpassing value of
knowing Christ Jesus my Lord, for whom I have suffered
the loss of all things, and count them but rubbish
in order that I may gain Christ" Phil. 3: 8

Once that barrier is taken down we can do everything that God may require of us. And what exactly is the barrier?

It is holding on to our own agenda.
It is holding on to our pleasures.
It is holding on to our earthly security.
It is holding on to our own reputation.
It is holding on to people's good opinion of us.
It is the unwillingness to look like a fool for the cause of Christ.

Jesus passed every one of these tests;

"He emptied Himself, taking the form of a bond-servant
and being made in the likeness of men.
And being found in appearance as a man, He humbled Himself
by becoming obedient to the point of death even death on
a cross." Phil. 2:7-8

His joy was the intimacy He shared with His Father and His reward was;

"Therefore also God highly exalted Him, and bestowed on Him the
name which is above every name, that at the name of Jesus
every knee should bow of those who are in heaven and on earth
and under the earth, and every tongue confess that Jesus Christ
is Lord to the glory of the Father." Phil. 2:9-11.

THE PASSIONS OF THE FLESH

Now we come to the next area of picking up our cross to follow Him. In the list we just reviewed, one of the items was holding on to our pleasures. That is what we'll tackle now. We'll explore two aspects of pleasures.

The first area to address is our passionate pleasures. These pleasures include all the animal appetites including food, drink, alcohol, smoking, music, entertainment and sex. Some areas such as use of street drugs or the misuse of prescription drugs are easily dealt with. Don't do it. Though some people who are just emerging from a lifestyle of drug abuse claim to have 'enlightened' moments on drugs and try to continue the practice while growing in God, it can't be done. If you want to grow in Christ, you must put away all that is of darkness. This goes for partying, drunkenness, immorality, worldly concerts etc. These are what we call gross sins, or sins that are so obviously wrong that we don't even need to discuss it. The words of Paul suffice:

"Now the deeds of the flesh are evident which are immorality,
impurity, sensuality, idolatry, sorcery, enmities, strife, jealousy,
drunkenness, carousing and things like these
of which I forewarn you, that those who practice those
things shall not inherit the kingdom of God." Gal. 5:19-21

"The night is almost gone and the day is at hand.
Let us therefore lay aside the deeds of darkness
and put on the armor of light. Let us behave properly
as in the day, not in carousing and drunkenness,
not in sexual promiscuity and sensuality,
But put on the Lord Jesus Christ and make no provision
for the flesh in regard to its lusts. Rom. 13:12-14.

"Our old self was crucified with Him that our body of sin might be
done away with, that we should no longer be slaves of sin;
for he who has died is freed from sin.
Even so consider yourselves to be dead to sin
but alive to God in Christ Jesus."

144

Therefore do not let sin reign in your mortal body
    that you should obey its lusts." Rom. 6:6-12.

Here we see clearly this concept that it is the cross of Christ that frees us from sin. It is being crucified with Him. This crucifixion is the ability to abstain from earthly lusts and passions. It is putting to death the desires that ran rampant in us before we met Jesus. What God is promising us here is that He will allow us the privilege and the strength to lay all these things aside. If we will give Him our will, that is, our determination to pursue these things, if we look up to heaven and say "Lord Jesus I don't know how I can live without these things, but I'm willing to let You clean them out of my life," that person will be granted the freedom and strength to stop. Many, many testimonies come forth from those who have been hopeless drug addicts and alcoholics. As they have given their lives to Christ, He has delivered them from their addictions. Such is the power of Christ. If you are struggling with some of these  things, as many are, the key is your will. Give your will over to God and tell Him you want to be obedient and follow after Him. That is a prayer He will always answer. If you can't bring yourself to that point yet, simply be honest and say "I want to follow You, please give me the *desire* to stop my sinful pursuits." He is gracious and will hear that cry as well.

The results of such prayers are wonderful! By picking up our cross to follow Jesus [in this case the desire to lay aside all our gross sins] we are being conformed to His death. That is, like Him we are putting away our own pleasures to do what is right. When we do that we also are joined with Him in His resurrection! We are lifted up and filled with true joy of living. Paul says,

"Therefore we have been buried with Him
    through baptism into death, in order that as
Christ was raised from the dead through the glory of the Father,
    so we too might walk in the newness of life.
For if we have become united with Him in the likeness of
His death certainly we shall be also in the
    likeness of His resurrection." Rom. 6:4-5.

LAWFUL PLEASURES

Once we have given God all our gross sins, He then begins a cleanup of the rest of our passions. First let's try to understand exactly what a passion is. We listed some of the passions and they included things like food. Now, since we must have food in order to live, how is that a passion? Good question!

God has granted us all types of lawful pleasures. In fact He made us and this whole wonderful universe for our pleasure and delight! The unending variety of foods and spices show us that He designed these things with us in mind. So God is not like the concept that was so prevalent during the dark ages, that if it's enjoyable, it's evil and we have to avoid it. Centuries of religious people have built their lives on abstaining from every pleasant thing. God takes no pleasure in withholding good from His children any more than a loving parent would take any kind of pleasure in setting out a beautiful meal before the children and then saying "I'm sorry but you can't have any of it." God delights in giving good things to His children!

EXCEEDING THE SPEED LIMIT

Unfortunately the problem enters with us [not surprisingly], because we enjoy those good things improperly. We take something good and we make something bad out of it. We do that simply by taking things too far. We make too much of our food, our drink, our music and our sex. What would be lawful within the limits that God has prescribed becomes unlawful when we go beyond those limits. Let's go back to the illustration of the speed limit because it perfectly and easily demonstrates lawful pleasures. Say you are driving along and you exceed the speed limit. Then because of your desire to feel the thrill of going fast, you end up getting an expensive ticket. Now you are devastated and determine that you can't ever drive again because the police are after you. Of course that's ridiculous, the police don't require you to stop driving, they simply require that you stay within the speed limit. If you obey that limit, you have freedom to enjoy driving whenever you want. So it is with all God's lawful pleasures. If they are enjoyed within the limits, they can be enjoyed with His blessing! If they are taken beyond the limits, we will pay the price for breaking the law.

When we go too far, a pleasure becomes a passion. The pleasure is legal; the passion is illegal. Why is a passion illegal? Because it has turned one of our desires into an idol - a false god that takes the place of the Living God. God desires us to be able to enjoy pleasures *in* Him, that is, with His blessing and with a spirit of thankfulness. This can be done as long as we enjoy things moderately. The moment we cross the line by letting it become a passion we no longer have His blessing and the passion begins to kill our soul. Peter sums it up:

> *"Beloved, I urge you as aliens and strangers [of this world] to*
> *abstain from fleshly lusts, which wage war against your soul."*
> *1 Peter 2:11*

Does that mean we can never enjoy anything again? Of course not, He just wants it to be lawful. That was the mistake the ascetics and monks made in the early days of Christianity and by it, ended up in various heresies such as combining Christianity with Stoicism.

WHAT IS THE SPEED LIMIT?

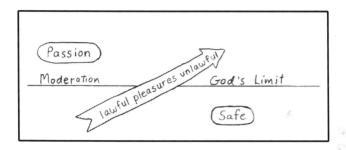

Of course now the question is, how do we know what the legal limits are to God? Well, in some cases it is clearly defined and in others we have to follow guidelines and principles.

Sex: In the case of sexual relations what are the legal boundaries? Sexual sin abounds in our society and the movie industry has become a virtual fountain of immorality. It is almost impossible to escape the perversion. The spirit of lust invades every corner of our world. Does that mean that sexual relations are wrong? Not at all. God made it to be a delight within the boundaries. He also set up guidelines to optimize our relations with our spouse. So what are the bounds?

First, it must be within the confines of legal mariage. There are no exceptions to this. There is no time when you can know in your heart that this time it's all right because you love each other and are committed.

Isn't God being a little too strict for our modern times? That standard couldn't possibly apply to us! Is it too strict that He doesn't want to see you a year from now with a little baby and no husband? God knows human nature and it is you He is trying to protect. No matter what your feelings are, sex cannot be legally enjoyed as an affair [adultery] or between two young people before marriage [fornication]. Believe God, this is for your good, not His!

Second, once you are married, your love life can be optimized by following His laws of love. Lust is a passion. Love is a virtue. Lust is going into relations [even with your wife or husband] thinking primarily of your own pleasure. He or she then becomes an object for your satisfaction. This is the most common condition in married couples today. This makes it a self-centered experience which your partner will find very unfulfilling. Don't think that just because you're married anything goes and you are free to indulge your lusts. Love is the law. Lust breaks the law and brings penalty. The penalty in this case is that it will also be unsatisfying for you! God is closer than you think and watches over all things.

To enter into love and have a lawful, God-blessed experience, all you must do is start thinking about the other person. Start to be concerned with giving him or her pleasure. Suddenly everything works. As you use yourself to bless your mate, you suddenly have sex being used properly and within God's laws. And God Himself will bless your time and make it wonderfully fulfilling for both of you!

Food: With food we must stick to principles because it can be different with each person. Lawful eating becomes unlawful gluttony when we exceed moderation. That unlawful limit can either be in the form of enjoying it passionately, excessive portions or excessive pickiness about the quality. That's where it becomes an individual thing. A hulking man could sit down to a huge steak with a helping of potatoes and not be gluttonous. A delicate looking woman could sit down to a tiny specially prepared meal and be guilty of sin. The difference is this - for the man, if he's worked hard all day, that could be just enough to comfortably fill him. For the woman, her portion could be ridiculously small but if she has terrorized her cook staff or the waiter because she can't eat it unless it's perfect, that person has gone over the limit.

God does not want us to make over much of our food. He wants us to enjoy it moderately if it's good and not complain if it's bad. Those are the guidelines.

EVERYTHING IN MODERATION

Regarding all the other pleasures, the key is this: Everything in moderation. Just think of the speed limit whenever you're indulging in something that is pleasurable to you. Music, videos, games, sports etc. are often areas that completely take over our lives. If it goes to excess you're breaking God's laws even though it is a lawful pleasure. So here again the key is the cross. Once God has rooted out the major sins of the flesh now He asks us to apply the cross to *all* areas of our life. He asks us to embrace moderation. That can be a difficult thing because we are a passionate people who are ruled by passions. In fact, we are slaves to our passions and can't escape.  So now, we must do as the drug addict and the alcoholic, we must look up to God and give Him our will in the matter. We must give Him those areas that are out of order and ask Him to bring them under control. If we can't do that with our heart, we must simply take one step back and ask Him to give us the *desire* to make these things right. He will actually come to you and give you miraculous help. He knows already that we can't stop sinning; all He's looking for is our willingness to be made clean.

OUR PLEASURE IS WHERE OUR HEART IS

These things are very important because our pleasures determine where our heart is. Whatever our pleasures are that's where our thoughts and interests are. If our pleasure lies in any of the passions of the flesh that is a true reflection of our condition in Christ. These things are our true gods, they are what we live for: then added to that we may also have an interest in Jesus and being saved. God is off to the side. He is only *one* of our interests. By taking up the cross we must follow God's word in putting to death all the passions of the flesh. One by one we must surrender them. God is patient and simply proceeds methodically through our life to make it clean and white. The moment we stop allowing Him to clean us in an area, that's where we stop in our walk with Jesus. I have seen many times where a person has made great strides in being cleaned from all the gross sins after becoming born-again, only to be stopped dead by refusing to allow God to clean out their pet passion. Of course this reluctance only comes from a lack of knowledge. They fear, like the silly motorist, that if once they surrender that area to God they will never have it again. And it's too dear to them, so they're afraid to let it go. No, God only wants to make it lawful. He may indeed take it away for a season, but He will return it to you in its good and lawful form once you've let Him have it.

NOTHING BUT CHRIST

We might be tempted to think that if we give up all these things to follow Christ, we will have nothing left but Him. That's exactly what our goal is: *nothing but Christ!* We *want* to put all things into subjection to Him and we *want* to give Him preeminence in all! We don't want any passions or idols to come between us and our Beloved Savior. Christ is to become our life. Then, *"When Christ who is our life is revealed, you also will be revealed with Him in glory." Col. 3:4*

The process of becoming dead to all the passions of the flesh is a long, slow ordeal which requires taking up our cross daily to follow Him. The fruit of all those tiny choices becomes a rich harvest! As we sell all we own to obtain the Pearl of Great Price, He becomes ours! The Lord Himself becomes our delight and our most exquisite pleasure. And as we mentioned before, there is no pleasure on earth that can compare to the heavenly delights which are granted to those who are close to Him. The Psalmist says it well in Psalm 73:25-28,

"Whom have I in heaven but Thee?
And besides Thee, I desire nothing on earth.
My flesh and my heart may fail,
But God is the strength of my heart and my portion forever.
But as for me, the nearness of God is my good."

In all these things we can truly say - this is the narrow gate, the surprising door to a radiant life.

150

LESSON 22

LAYING ASIDE EVERY ENCUMBRANCE

We now come to the heart of our mission - real revival begining with us! It is not just to be content to face persecution and resistance with steadfastness, or to put away the gross sins of the flesh. Nor is it content to subject the passions of our earthly appetites. Our goal is nothing less than following the words of Hebrews 12:1-2,

> *"Therefore since we have so great a cloud of witnesses*
> *surrounding us, let us also lay aside every encumbrance*
> *and the sin which so easily entangles us, and let us run*
> *with endurance the race that is set before us.*
> *Fixing our eyes on Jesus the author and perfecter of faith,*
> *who for the joy set before Him endured the cross,*
> *despising the shame and has sat down at the right hand of*
> *the throne of God."*

In addition to all the sin which so easily entangles us there are also encumbrances. *An encumbrance is as good as a sin for slowing us down in our walk with Jesus.* What exactly is an encumbrance? It is a distraction, anything that distracts us from following God. This opens up a whole new category of our lives to scrutiny. For besides being filled up with every type of sinful lust and passion, all the remainder of our time is usually occupied by distractions!

DISTRACTIONS

What qualifies as a distraction? Anything that turns our thoughts away from God. For some it could be as small as reading the Sunday paper, for others it could be being employed by a high-powered firm that saps all their time and energy. Here's a scary thought - many will be distracted out of the Kingdom of Heaven by nothing more than a hand-held cellular device! For all, though, worldly entertainment quali- fies as a bonifide distraction. Your enemy, the devil, does not care one bit what means he uses so long as he can distract your attention from God! Of course, he's always glad to pull people into the pit by getting them strung out on drugs or alcohol. And he still takes great pleasure in luring a young woman away by using an ungodly boyfriend. But he has other methods that are equally effective in turning people from God. If they are already church-going Christians, plunk them down in front of the TV at night and he has completely neutralized any threat of them growing close to God!! If he can get Christians to be talking about and anticipating the latest movie releases - wow! What could be better? If he can get God's people to spend their free time playing the same video games as their worldly neighbors - how much better can it get?

We can all put different labels on, but when the holy God looks down upon the sons of men, can He see light and darkness among the people or is it just one big gray mass? Has the Christian church become so involved with worldly entertainment that it ceases to be the salt and light that preserves the world? In North America, unfortunately the answer to that is for the most part, yes. We bring God no pleasure when we fill our thoughts with all the input of the world. We cease to bring Him joy when all day long we listen to secular music, watch ungodly movies and play captivating games which deaden us to the realities of God and involve us in all things demonic. Then we try to convince Him that everything is okay because we go to church or youth group! Entertainment is the snare which has been carefully designed to capture those who have made an outward profession of faith. And our enemy howls with laughter! He doesn't care that we are free from alcohol abuse or drugs or that we outwardly lead a good life. It makes no difference to him whatever because anything that distracts us from Christ is of equal value to him!!

THE BEGGAR PRINCE

In ancient times an evil druid seethed with hatred toward a certain nobleman. The nobleman's wealth and power however prohibited any means of effectively warring against him. So the druid's cunning mind devised a cruel and devious plan to hurt his rival to the quick without armed confrontation. Amidst his orbs

and candles he muttered an incantation and cast a wicked spell upon the *son* of the nobleman.

The following day as the child was brought to the city he began to have a strange fascination with all that was around him. All the sights and sounds seemed to captivate him. He became so engrossed that he forgot what he was doing and slipped away unnoticed into the crowd. There he met some beggar children and after being mocked for his finery, took his royal garments off and laid them aside. Soon he began playing games with the street children, running, hiding, eating stolen fruit until the spell of the druid worked its wicked magic and the boy completely forgot who he was. He neither remembered where he was from nor who his father was. Eventually he became as one of the street urchins - grubby, poverty stricken and completely obsessed with the small mean pleasures of the beggars. Where he had once dined with crystal and fine china he now sought a few beans dropped into his filthy hands.

His father was grief stricken and daily conducted searches of the towns and countryside, but the child's appearance was so altered as

to make recognition nearly impossible. One day the royal carriage passed by with his family crest on it. As the boy stared it seemed to mean something to him but it eluded him. He strained to remember the meaning of those symbols, but at that moment he became distracted by a marionette playfully calling to him from a street theater. The fog then closed back over his mind and he resumed his pastimes without another glance back.

Unfortunately, this story can't have a happy ending, because it hasn't ended yet. That child is you and me. We have an enemy who hates us merely because he passionately hates our Father. He has fashioned a spell over our minds to make us forget who we are, what we are doing and who our Father is. His spell is in the form of the passing pleasures of this world (1 John 2:15-17) and the idle distractions that cause us to do just one thing, forget. The son in this story would have been joyously received, clothed in fine garments and given a high place of responsibility if he would only remember who he was.

More than ever before we live in an age where we are distracted to forget who we are in Christ. The devil has placed magic in those passing pleasures. They seem so enticing, so irresistible. They are beautiful sparkly baubles put in front of us to draw us away. Some seem harmless and not even sinful but all serve to distract us. Every now and then something will come  along, like the carriage with the family crest. It will be a scripture or a message that will stir us a little. We'll get uncomfortable and feel like we're starting to remember; then suddenly we'll be distracted by the next release of our favorite game or movie. Then the fog closes in again. Once again we forget who we are, that we have a high calling and that we have a special Father.

If the young man in the story never remembered who he was, he would end up dying a beggar. In the same way if we follow the normal course and fill our lives with the pleasures and pursuits of the world, we will die beggars. 1 John 2: 16-17 says; *"for all that is in the world, the lust of the flesh, the lust of the eyes and the boastful pride of life is not from the father but from the world. And the world is passing away and also its lusts, but the one who does the will of the father abides forever."*

 But if the son remembers who he is, he will immediately be received, washed, dressed and given a responsible position. So our hardest work isn't the accomplishment of some goal in sports or scholastics, it is the diligent remembering of whose child we are in the midst of the City of Destruction. That is no small task because the devil hates you and devises an infinite number of distractions to snare you. It's a full time job to keep our sights on God, but the reward is immeasurable. Those who give in to the temptation of exciting distractions find that instead of excitement and pleasure, they end up with a dull, drab life of complete emptiness and despair. Those who stay faithful and watchful, begin drinking pure water from

the River of Delights and in the end, will have riches, honor, contentment, fulfillment and will inherit eternal life. Let us remember who our Father is, that our family crest is the cross and let it remind us that we have a high and noble calling as true sons and daughters of the King!

YOUR THOUGHTS DETERMINE YOUR RELATIONSHIP

As we begin to see the dangers that are inherent to worldly entertainment and distractions, it is our goal to offer assistance to those who decide that their eternal souls are worth whatever the price is to ensure their safety. These distractions are the greatest threat to your relationship with God, because your thoughts are determined by the input you have during the day. Your thoughts determine what your relationship with God is. If your input is from the radio at work and from the TV and computer at night these sources will provide your thought life. Scary, isn't it? Now take this test for yourself:

THE TEST

Think carefully about how much secular, ungodly input you get during the course of a day from music, movies, TV, computers, newspapers, magazines and people around you. Next consider how much Godly input you get in a day from reading the Bible, studying, stimulating conversation and Godly entertainment. It makes you think doesn't it? If you are an average Christian in the western hemisphere you probably receive at least 10 hours or more of actual ungodly input during a day. During that same day you probably don't receive *any* Godly input. Godly input is reserved for church on Sunday and the occasional midweek service. Even if you are 'involved' with your church, how much time do you spend seeking God on your own and how much of your church time is in 'activities' as opposed to actually focused on the lessons of Jesus? Probably very little.

THE SEED

Let us consider that everything we see or read or listen to acts like a little seed that is planted into our life. Those seeds grow up and produce a harvest that is of the same nature as the seed. Like produces

155

like. Now let's consider that these seeds come up slowly, not overnight so that the evidence of the type of seed is not seen for a period of years. What type of harvest can you expect to see? Let's carefully consider the words of Paul in Galations 6:7-8,

"For do not be deceived, God is not mocked,
for whatever a man sows that he will also reap.
For the one who sows to his own flesh,
shall from the flesh reap corruption.
But the one who sows to the Spirit
shall from the Spirit reap eternal life."

Every day from the time we wake up until we go to bed we are planting seeds. We are either sowing to the flesh or we are sowing to the Spirit. There is no middle ground and no way to just exist. At all times we are sowing seeds. God's Word will not be mocked and will not return void. It is unfailing and unstoppable. So all that we do in the course of a day is either filling us with corruption or it's filling us with holiness. We are indeed like the young man in the story, because our distractions serve to make us forget these very words and scriptures we are discussing right now! Even now these words may be provoking some uncomfortable thoughts because deep inside we know they are right. But, we are so steeped in our pastimes that it seems too hard to think about. All it will take for some is to go home and pop on a movie and all the discomfort will leave. You will completely forget that your soul is at stake. Remember the marionette. It is so much easier to relax than to cling to the knowledge of the truth.

"Enter by the narrow gate, for the gate is wide
and the way is broad that leads to destruction,
and many are those who enter by it.
For the gate is small and the way is narrow
that leads to life." Matt. 7:13-14.

The pleasures, comforts and pastimes of this world pleasantly numb us to all that pertains to God. It is the broad way that leads to destruction. It makes the things of God seem far away and difficult to obtain. They act the same as sin, because they get a hold of us and won't let go. As we mentioned a distraction is every bit as good as a sin because both keep us from seeking God. And seek God we must if we value our soul. If we have, like most others, been planting years and years of bad seed, we can expect to reap the harvest of corruption. That corruption is already at work in us to make the things of God foggy and unclear. It has already worked its evil magic into every part of our life and thoughts. We are hopelessly ensnared and can't get out without the supernatural intervention of Jesus. It requires that we earnestly seek Him as though our very lives depended on it.

THE FELLOWSHIP OF THE UNASHAMED

Our fellowship is nothing more than a group of people who are concerned enough about their relationship with God to do something radical about it. Each one has decided that whatever the cost is, *his soul is worth it*. If it means becoming out of touch with the latest movie releases, fine. If it means becoming totally different from everyone around you, that's why it's called the Unashamed.

> *"For whoever is ashamed of Me and My words*
> *in this adulterous and sinful generation,*
> *The Son of Man will also be ashamed of him when*
> *He comes in the glory of the Father with*
> *the holy angels." Mark 8:38*

Each one in the Fellowship of the Unashamed has made a commitment to seek God earnestly and the commitment includes two parts. The first is to stop planting bad seed that produces corruption; the second is to start planting good seed that results in eternal life. We will discuss the first part now and the second in another lesson.

157

THE COMMITMENT

The commitment to stop planting bad seed includes the truly radical step of eliminating worldly input from our lives for as much as it is in our power to do so. I personally know those who have disposed of their TVs, disconnected or sold their game equipment, eliminated their secular music collection and stopped going to movies. Now *there* is a group who is serious about their relationship with Jesus! Can you imagine how delighted their Savior is with them? Can you think how pleasing that is to Him? His children have just become salty and full of light! We in the West do not face persecution like our brothers and sisters in other countries, but we do have to make the same radical commitment to God. We have to decide to follow Christ no matter what the cost. If worldly entertainment is deadening your soul, then the price of being a disciple is getting rid of it. Halleluia!

If you think that is going too far and demanding too much consider these scriptures:

"This is pure and undefiled religion in the sight of our
God and Father, to visit orphans and widows in their distress
and to keep oneself unstained by the world." James 1:27

The Psalmist takes it even farther by saying,

"I will walk within my house in the integrity of my heart.
I will set no worthless thing before my eyes;
I hate the work of those who fall away.
It shall not fasten its grip on me." Psalm 101:2-3.

IT SHALL NOT FASTEN ITS GRIP ON ME

These words speak directly to us and should be our standard. Our walk with God is corrupted right within our home. It is compromised by every minute of worldly entertainment we subject our souls to. So it is exciting to obey this word! It is victorious

to put aside the worthless things we set before our eyes. The psalmist goes further to the point by saying he hates the work of those who fall away. How clearly does this speak to us? It gives us the courage and strength to stand up and say "Wait, I don't care who the actor and director of the latest blockbuster is, I hate the work of those who fall away! I'm not going to forfeit my soul or my relationship with Jesus for the work of someone who has no knowledge of eternal life! Why should I *'follow the multitude in sin' [Ex. 23:2]* just because everyone else is." And so we make a stand. It is a stand that will cost you the scorn of some friends, but what is that in exchange for eternal life? It may initially cost us a little discomfort as we give up one of our greatest pleasures. But isn't Jesus worth it? Yes, we are glad to sell all to obtain the Pearl of Great Price.

Notice, also, the words of the psalmist using the same language to describe our entanglement with these things. He says "It shall not fasten its grip on me." That is precisely what we mean when we say these pleasures deaden us and cause us to lose sight of those things which are vitally important to us. There is almost no one in America who is not struggling in this matter. The worthless things we set before our eyes have fastened their grip on us.

LESSON 23

SSSHHH, SLEEPING VIRGINS!

VARIOUS END TIME SCENARIOS

Because of the warehouses of books that have theorized about the last days, most modern minds are not overly worried that the end times will catch them off guard. We all privately think that we are basically aware of what's going on and that we will be prepared when the time comes. Based on the popular books, we will see certain obvious 'signs of the times' that would indeed be hard to miss even by the most casual Christians. Unfortunately, the theories are built on passages of scripture that use what is called 'prophetic imagery.' Even those who claim to be strict 'literalists' admit that we probably won't see an actual ten horned beast rise up from the ocean. Because of the allegorical nature of prophetic imagery, it is prudent to not be dogmatic in our interpretation of the end times [though in fact almost everyone is]. We see from the previously fulfilled prophecies of Daniel that all the images seen in his visions related to certain kings and kingdoms. So the unfulfilled scenes may also have a more natural fulfillment that could be hard to see at the moment. Since there are almost as many interpretations as there are interpreters, it is better for us to stick to safe ground. And what is the safe ground? I can think of none safer than the words of Jesus Himself. Therefore, we will take a rather unique stand by putting heavy emphasis on the descriptions of the last days found in the *gospels*.

THE GOSPELS TAKE PRECEDENCE

Jesus warns us repeatedly in the Gospels that the greatest danger during the last days is that His people, the church, will fall asleep. Surprisingly, He doesn't say they will fall away because of persecution, He says many will be asleep when He returns. The wakeful bride will go in with Him and all the rest will be shut outside. These are clear passages. There are many of them and yet for some reason they are almost completely ignored by the experts of the end times. The more obscure passages, however, are widely quoted.

160

Let's examine the passage concerning the 10 sleeping virgins. Because it is lengthy, I will summarize it while you follow along in Matt. 25:1-13.

THE TEN VIRGINS

Ten virgins [symbolizing the church], go out to meet the bridegroom [Jesus]. Half took extra oil with them for their lamps while the other half assumed they would only be a short while and therefore figured no extra oil was needed. While they were waiting, the bridegroom delayed. As the hours wore on they all got drowsy and fell asleep. Suddenly there was a shout. He was coming! Those with their lamps still burning went out to meet him and those whose lamps had gone out missed him. The bridegroom took those who were ready in with him to the wedding feast. Eventually, the rest came  with their lamps refilled, but it was too late. In response to their frantic calls, the bridegroom answered that he did *not even know them.*

The message in this parable contains two distinct parts. One is that they needed to have endurance as they waited for their beloved *[those who endure to the end shall be saved].* Jesus is referring to this when He talks about the oil for their lamps. They had to have the perseverance necessary to be ready all the way to the very end when He comes. The second part, which is what we'll focus on, is that they all became drowsy and fell asleep. This warning to be on the alert is the most prominent part of Jesus' teaching on the last days. He mentions it again in Mark 13: 32-33 and in many other places;

> *"But of that day and that hour no one knows, not even*
>   *the angels in heaven nor the Son, but the Father alone.*
> *Take heed, keep on the alert for you do not know*
>   *when the appointed time is.*

In fact in the entire gospel of Mark, the warning of being awake and alert is Jesus' only exhortation on the matter of His second coming. He tells us not to be caught asleep after He warns us that everyone will be drowsy!

NO SNOOZING

What does Jesus mean when He says 'asleep,' since He is obviously not referring to it in literal sense? The sleep that He is warning us against is spiritual sleep - that means asleep to the things of God. The apostle Paul also describes sleep as spiritual degeneracy. He speaks of the same issue in 1 Thes. 5:2,6,7,

> *"For you yourselves know full well that the day of the*
> *Lord will come just like a thief in the night."*
> *"So then let us not sleep as others do but*
> *let us be on the alert and sober.*
> *For those who sleep do their sleeping at night and*
> *those who get drunk get drunk at night."*

So here we have an accurate picture of sleep. It is deadness towards the things of God. What are some of the things we know about sleep?

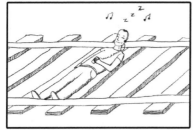 Well, ask anyone who has fallen asleep during one of my lessons! Sleep comes upon you in an undetectable way. It is so irresistible that when you are under its influence you can think of nothing else. When we hear of the virgins becoming drowsy we all know what a horrible feeling it is if you are supposed to stay alert. It is very familiar to us all when we are attending a particularly long lecture class or while we are driving home late at night. We know it is vitally important that we stay awake and yet the urge to close our eyes for just a second is overwhelming! If we can think of our waiting for Jesus to be the same as that long drive late at night, we will have a pretty good picture of how important it is to stay alert. Our life depends on it. Because of the extreme consequences of falling asleep, we take every precaution against it. We stop often, we walk in the cold air, we stop for coffee, we open the window. We earnestly fight to stay awake because we must. As we wait for our Blessed Savior to return we must have the same urgency. We must always keep at the front of our minds that not only our life, but our eternal spiritual life depends on it! Then we must do everything necessary to prevent sleep from overtaking us.

THE ROAD TRIP

Picture riding down the road at 2:00 AM by yourself, driving to meet the one you love. As the late night wears on your eyelids start to drift down and you are startled awake by your head bobbing. So you try to focus a little harder on the road. You decide to take a break and get a good meal. You stop at a roadside diner and decide on a huge chicken dinner with all the sides. After finishing that off along with the diner's specialty, apple pie a la mode, you head back out to the open road. As your great dinner begins to digest, not surprisingly you start to get drowsy again. Meanwhile, you have the radio turned to a station that is playing pleasant, hypnotic music. It's so captivating that it's almost disorienting. It fills the car with an irresistible urge to fall asleep. You also have turned down the dashboard lights so they won't shine so brightly in your eyes. And you notice that there is no one on the road at that hour, so there are no lights whatever to disturb you. Besides this, you've brought some 'aroma therapy' incense which you light and put in the ash tray. You just love the fragrance as it makes a heavy cloud of perfume. Last but not least, your back is starting to bother you from all the driving. So you reach into the back seat and pull out a special pillow designed to make you quite comfortable while you drive. Now you're set to drive all night!

ASLEEP AT THE WHEEL

Given those conditions, it is almost certain that you will *not* make it safely to your destination. Now it may seem absurd when we look at that picture, but that is exactly what we are doing right now as we are driving towards our destination of meeting Jesus. We have a long way to go and so we prepare ourselves with all the comforts necessary to make the trip as enjoyable as possible. We have the radio going nicely in the background, which helps us forget how long the trip is. We stop often for a huge, truly delicious breakfast, lunch and dinner as we continue on our way. We have thought of everything for this trip! We have a little computer screen mounted so we can constantly monitor the internet. We have a headset to listen to our favorite music and talk to our friends. We have spared no expense and pleasure because after all, it is a long trip. In fact we are so comfortable that sometimes it doesn't even feel like we are going anywhere! As the hour gets later, it 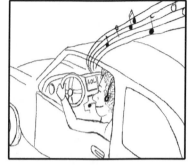 gets darker and darker. Meanwhile outside there are danger signs posted and detour signs. We fly right past the first set of warnings. We continue with no worries or concerns. While we pass the second warning, we are rummaging through our extensive music collection and miss it. In the pleasure of driving with the music going and the computer on and a phone call on the headset, we go right through the final barrier and crash in a fiery ball.

This is not a very pleasant picture, but it is a road that many of us are on. While we are busy with our distractions, we are missing some very important road signs. If we happen to see any lights [that is any scripture or sermon for example] that make us uncomfortable, we complain they are too bright and we turn them off! We have anything and everything that can possibly distract us from the job at hand surrounding us on all sides. Every gadget, gizmo, electronic toy, earthly comfort and worldly pleasure we have packed right in with us. Unfortunately, like the person in our story, we will have a very slim chance of making it safely to our destination, which is to meet the Bridegroom.

STAYING ALERT

Rather, those who are intent upon staying awake conduct themselves in a much different fashion than the one in this story, thereby saving their own lives and safely meeting their loved one. Instead of surrounding themselves with all the bodily comforts which will inevitably lead to drowsiness, they purposefully engage in activities that will make the body uncomfortable. They buffet their physical body as the Apostle Paul calls it in order to stay awake and alert. Rather than listening to [spiritually] sleep-inducing music, they turn it off and begin to sing out loud the psalms, hymns and spiritual songs that will cause their spirit to wake up. Sound too drastic to you? Your life is at stake! The things that lull your spiritual senses to sleep will not only cause you to go off the road and be killed but will cause you to plunge right over the cliff into the abyss of hell. Just consider how serious the statement is that Jesus makes when He says the remainder of the virgins are barred from entering the marriage feast. *These are people that started out to follow the Lord. These are not wicked sinners. These could be good-hearted Christian people that have been entertained to death.* While they drive on toward the destination of meeting Jesus, their only crime is that they are distracted by all the world's entertainment and it makes them sleepy to the things of God. What a horrible way to end a promising beginning!

So as the hour gets later, we must resort to more and more drastic measures to keep our eyes on the road. Turn the music off. Turn the computer off. Open the window all the way. Sing out loud. Get rid of the cushy pillows. Don't fill yourself with fine food and alcohol. Keep your eyes wide open. Do whatever it takes to make yourself uncomfortable. I love the example of brother George Whitfield. His method of keeping spiritually alert was to sleep on top of the ship deck instead of in a soft birth! Remember the goal is to arrive safely!

THE PARABLE OF THE SOILS

So we see that despite our good intentions, the great trial of the last days will be spiritual alertness in the midst of many distractions that will lull us to sleep spiritually. Jesus gives us insight into the various distractions that can cause us to leave the road. In Matthew chapter 13 He tells us the parable of the seed being sown in different types of soil. It is a lesson which shows how potentially good seed can become ultimately worthless simply by allowing the worldly distractions to choke it out. Assuming that everyone knows this parable [if not, read it in Matt. 13: 3 - 30], we will focus on the third soil type mentioned, the seed that fell among the thorns.

This soil represents good seed that fell on essentially good soil. That means He is addressing those who are Christians and have a love for God. The only problem is that there are thorns among the seeds. These thorns cause the seed to become unfruitful.

"And the one on whom seed was sown among thorns,
this is the man who hears the word,

and the worry of the world and the deceitfulness of riches
choke the word and it becomes unfruitful."

Here Jesus clearly shows us the temptations that will cause deadness. They are simply all the common pressures and distractions of daily life and the deceitfulness of riches. It is interesting to note that we currently live in an age that is obsessed with riches. It may seem normal to us who live at this time, but it is hard to find a period in history which has so totally abandoned true values for the sake of making money. We now promote music and movies on the basis of only one criteria - if it sells, it's good; if it doesn't, it's bad. The moral content is not even considered. So top executives sell the souls of their very own children for the sake of making money!

Because we live in the world, we are constantly tempted to worry about all that the world worries about - investments, percentage points, etc. But, we are to be *in* the world not *of* the world. We are to be good and wise stewards, but we're managing God's money, not ours. There's a big difference there. If we think of it as our money, we will fall into the snare mentioned in this parable. We will be drawn away by the deceitfulness of riches. Rather we are to do as Paul urges us in Corinthians - handle the world as though we handled it not. That means keeping an arms length away from the entanglements of the pursuit of money. Money is to live; we don't live for money. We must be separated from the world's mentality, reserving our love and affection not for pagan idols of gold or silver, but for the living God.

THE WORKING MOM

The other thorns mentioned by Jesus are also very important to consider. He says the fruit will be choked out by the worries and anxieties of life. This addresses a whole separate matter. For young people or those who have jobs which allow for leisure time, the greatest soul killing distractions are electronic games and entertainment. For those who live with the harsh realities of life it's a whole different story. Many a working mother or single parent has no time to worry about the sinfulness of their pastimes. They have no pastimes! They work from the moment they awake until they collapse into bed at night. Their days are filled with demands and pressures and they often feel they're sinking into a hopeless bog of quicksand. No, they don't worry about too much TV! They are sacrificing every moment of their life for the sake of providing food and shelter for their family. As hard as this might sound, the devil doesn't care how he distracts us as long as he does distract us. That means he can use drugs and alcohol to sidetrack young people, entertainment to anesthetize church go-ers and for those who are hard-working and responsible, he can use their own responsibility against them! To show the effectiveness of this ploy just consider how many hard pressed mothers forsake going to church or studying the Bible because they are too busy! There simply

isn't enough time! And so the worries and anxieties of this life choke out the seed and it becomes unfruitful. The devil doesn't care if it's hard work that keeps you away from a close relationship with God. We are all in the same danger. We are all faced with distractions that cause us to forget God.

For working mothers I say this: God loves your determination to do the right thing by caring for your family. His heart is for you because He sees the struggles you go through. He also is mindful of your frame, that you are very often overcome by waves of anxiety. He intimately cares about the difficulties of your life. But let's heed the admonition which He gave to Martha. While He was teaching at her home, Martha came up to Him and complained that there was so much to do. Her sister, Mary, was listening to the words of Jesus and so was not helping out. Jesus gently rebuked Martha for her busyness and said that Mary had chosen the better part [Luke 10:38-42]. That means that no matter how pressing the concerns are around you, Jesus is also telling you to choose the better part. Setting aside time to be with the great Lover of your soul will do far more to settle your family affairs than all your hectic rushing. Put-ting God first in your life, making time

for church and Bible study will put all of God's great resources on your side. He will help you!

THE DAYS OF NOAH

"And just as it happened in the days of Noah,
so it shall also be in the days of the Son of Man.
They were eating, they were drinking, they were marrying,
they were being given in marriage, until the day
that Noah entered the ark and the flood came
and destroyed them all." Luke 17:26-27

Jesus' teaching on the end times as we see here in Luke 17, flies in the face of nearly every theory in every branch of the Christian church. Jesus Himself says that in the time preceding His coming, the world will be eating, drinking and marrying like in the days of Noah. They will be buying, selling, planting and building. It will be life as normal except that the world will be extraordinarily caught up in the pursuits of the world.

This is a serious warning to us and this lesson is devoted to sounding the alarm in order to wake the sleeping bride of Christ. It adds emphasis to the parable of the soils, by telling us outright that the last days will be characterized by worldly pursuits. The very issues mentioned in that parable, all the cares of life and the chasing after wealth, are now stated plainly as the distractions which will cause great and small to be swept away at His coming. No prophetic imagery here! We must be on the alert! Be honest with yourself because no one else will pay the consequences but you. Do you build your life around your boat, your motorcycle, your car, your home, your furnishings, your cottage, your electronic gadgets, your state of the art phone, your clothes or a combination of all the above? In an appalling survey mentioned in a popular magazine, when men were asked what was the most important thing in their life, more than half answered their *car!* That is a truly sad commentary on our society. Because that is the prevailing mind set, do you fall into it too? Are you influenced by the unchecked rush for worldly goods and toys? If you live in this world you probably are. This is the time to wake up, shake the cobwebs off your head and remember Jesus. He is coming back and His reward and punishment are with Him. He gives clear warning of the impending doom awaiting those Christians and non-Christians who have traded their eternal inheritance for the passing pursuits of this world.

THE DAYS OF LOT

Though we mentioned it earlier we will go back to the illustration of Lot's wife because it is the very next thing mentioned by Jesus in the Gospel of Luke;

"It was the same as happened in the days of Lot:
they were eating they were drinking, they were buying,
They were selling, they were planting, they were building;
but on the day that Lot went out from Sodom it rained
fire and brimstone from heaven and destroyed them all.
It will be just the same on the day that the Son of Man
is revealed." Luke 17:28-30

After stating the relative normalcy of the world just before He returns, Jesus gives us this cryptic message:

"Remember Lot's wife. Whoever seeks to keep his life will lose it
and whoever loses his life shall preserve it." Luke 17:32-33

At first glance it seems to simply reinforce one of the end time scenarios where believers must be strong in the face of persecution during a period of very recognizable persecution. But if we remember Lot's wife in the context of the story, we see that she was not running away to save her spiritual life, she was seeking to save her earthly life in Sodom. Her sin was not so much in the looking back, it was looking back with *regret*. She lamented leaving all the good things of her life behind in the city. God had gone very far out of His way to save her life, even to the point of delaying the impending disaster until she was safely away. And rather than having gratitude for her life being spared, she had regret that she was losing so much! She was caught up in the spirit of the place - buying, selling and building.

This is a great lesson for us. Anyone who has been through a boom time knows what a heady thing it is. People lose all sight of reality and are consumed with the good things of this life and making money. The time right before Jesus' return may be just like that. In fact He says it will be. It may be a heady time where people are exhilarated with the prospect of wealth and all its trimmings. It will be the spirit of the age and no one will be immune. Do we see these things now? Emphatically, yes. Is it a sign of His near return? Possibly. Jesus is warning us not about the fear of losing our physical life but the fear of losing our *carnal* lives. If we try to save our earthly ambitions we will end up losing our eternal life. These are very sobering words in the midst of a society filled with giddiness. So the great lesson of His coming is to be on the alert, alert to life in Christ. We are not to be caught asleep, that is, caught up in the pursuits of this world. That is why He will say to the sleepy virgins, "I never knew you." Those who use the name of God but serve the interests and pleasures of this present age, actually never did know the true God.

TIP-TOEING AROUND THE VIRGINS

Unfortunately despite all Jesus' warnings, for the most part the church is very careful to do everything *except* wake up the sleeping bride. You'll find preachers everywhere who do anything to keep their people from being alerted to any possible danger in their lukewarm lifestyle. You'll hear countless sermons on our assurance of salvation, that He loves us just as we are. As long as we slipped our hand up while every head was bowed and every eye was closed we are safe. Our commitment to Christ seems to end right there. We can stay right in our comfortable worldly lifestyle without any interference at all in many churches. Or you'll hear an infinite number of sermons on how God wants to bless us with an extravagant earthly lifestyle. And so the naive are carefully left in their slumbering state. This is the essence of the new gospel so prevalent today - come as you are and stay as you are. No change required.

This is not the conversion we see in the scriptures. When someone in the Bible is converted, he undergoes a radical transformation. He is changed. And so throughout history, we see those who find Christ become an unstoppable force in this world, going forth to do exploits in His name, even to the laying down of their own lives.

DON'T BE OFFENSIVE

But, we are guilty of tiptoeing also. How many times do we have an opportunity to speak up for Christ only to find that we don't want to be offensive? We hope 'they will see our light' instead. So we go on our way without saying a word. We've just quietly walked around someone in such a way as to not wake them up. We wouldn't want to cause them alarm!

We here in the Fellowship of the Unashamed must be just that - unashamed. Rather than walking lightly so we don't offend anyone, we must go forth with boldness and wake up everyone we can. We must be willing to do as Lot did. He went and woke up his sons-in-law in the middle of the night to tell them that the city was about to be destroyed [Gen. 19:14] . The Bible says that it seemed like foolishness to them. He was compelled by his concern for them to do something that seemed ridiculous to them. He did what had to be done. When they wouldn't listen, they perished in fire and brimstone.

We must likewise be compelled by our concern for others. We must emphatically try to rouse people from their worldly distractions in order to save their lives. We are told that after the Titanic was damaged the crew went frantically through the halls to warn the passengers. However, rather than raise alarm, they found the majority of people thought that the ship couldn't possibly go down! People proceeded nonchalantly to see what the commotion was about. Most went to a watery grave.

What we must remember is that just because the passengers

didn't believe there was danger didn't excuse the crew from doing everything in their power to save them. Part of the crew was rescued and we can only hope that they had peace of conscience that they had done everything possible to warn of the danger. Likewise, even though we might be saved, we will also want the assurance that we did everything we could to rescue the perishing.

LESSON 24

HOLDING FAST TO THE WORD OF LIFE

"Fight the good fight of faith;
Take hold of the eternal life
To which you were called"
1 Tim. 6:12

'THE PIT'
[a story]

Millennia ago, the father and mother of a race were created by the Maker. The world was full of light and beauty and glory. They were wonderfully happy in their enjoyment of the good things around them and especially in the Maker himself. The Maker, more like a father, out of concern for the safety of his creation, instructed them carefully to stay within the boundaries he had set. Nothing at all could hurt them so long as they stayed within the perimeter of their lovely garden.

Unfortunately, the Maker had an archenemy who could take no greater pleasure than destroying the creations in which he delighted so. The best way to hurt him was to hurt his children. So one day he  laid a careful trap. The Enemy stood just outside the boundary of the delightful garden where they lived and addressed them saying, "Look, it's perfectly safe to come over here, there is no danger!" And indeed it did look perfectly safe. And there were all sorts of interesting things to see. The enemy persisted, "You have been cooped up in that little garden too long. It's time to explore! It's time you were able to decide for yourself where you want to live!" Gingerly they took first one step then another over the boundary until they were actually outside the garden. Unknown to them, the enemy had concealed a huge pit that lay between them. Because it was covered with fronds and leaves the naive creatures had no way of knowing the danger that lie ahead. As they continued on in their new-found independence, to their dismay, they felt the ground suddenly give way. In another moment they fell right through the camouflage and plunged into the pit.

Immediately they were surrounded by cold, inky blackness. This dark hole was actually a huge cavern where the enemy himself lived. As the man and woman felt their way about they found to their great alarm there was no way out! The sides were wet and slippery. Worst of all, they were confined in the presence of the hideous enemy who had deceived them to their own ruin. Their misery was overwhelming as they remembered the beauty and freshness of the garden they once called their home.

Eventually they were able to find just enough water, mushrooms  and fungus to live on and made the best of it. But they continually lamented their stupid disobedience that led to such misfortune. After awhile they started having children and grandchildren and as they in turn had children, the cavern was gradually filled with people. The difference, though, was that the children and children's children were *born* in the hole. They had never seen the real world and never seen daylight! Having known only the pit, they did not even know what it was like on the outside. In fact as time went on, most people stayed far away from the hole where they had first fallen. They lived in the dark recesses of the cave and never saw even the dim light at the top.

There were religious leaders of the various tribes and clans who were highly esteemed for their knowledge. These leaders had great positions of respect and they used it to lord it over the people. The leaders hated the hole with the dim light at the top. Whenever they got near it, the light exposed them to everyone. They had been in the dark places so long that they had grown horribly ugly and deformed. Therefore, they did everything in their power to keep their people away from the light.

After a time, the Maker put into effect a rescue plan to save his beloved creatures. He had been waiting until his people were truly sorry for their disobedience and ready to stay within the safety of his boundaries. When the moment finally arrived he sent his own son down into the very depths of the hole to bring them up! Multitudes

gathered to him to listen to his stories
about life outside the pit. They were cap-
tivated by its beauty and earnestly desired
to look upon the bright land with their
own eyes. But all this infuriated the religious leaders. They were losing their hold
over the people! As the crowds gathered
at the mouth of the pit and began to look
upwards, suddenly the enemy appeared in

their midst. Like a ravenous tiger he sprang upon the Maker's son!
With a vicious hatred he tore him to pieces. A few moments later
his lifeless form lay at the bottom of the hole.The crowds looked on
in dismay. Their rescuer was dead and all hope of getting out was
gone. The Enemy retreated back into his lair and the religious leaders
dispersed the people.

For three long gloomy days, darkness itself seemed to engulf every
nook and cranny of the cavern. Many just lay down where they were
as a tide of hopelessness swept over every living thing.

As those closest to the hole lay down, however, something ex-
traordinary happened. As they lay on their backs gazing upwards,
suddenly they saw someone's face peering over the opening. It was
their beloved rescuer leaning over the hole! He was alive! The Enemy
did not know that the Maker's son knew full well he would be killed
in the pit and had *willingly* gone to his death. By this supreme act
of love he had paid the penalty in full for the disobedience of all the
children. The Maker's son had stepped forward and taken the full
punishment in place of the rebellious children. Now he was beginning a massive evacuation of the pit! The just nature of the Maker
had caused his son to be miraculously restored to life and because
of his wonderful sacrifice he was given complete authority over the
enemy and freedom to lead the rescue mission!

Standing at the top of the hole, he let a thick rope down to them
saying "Grab tightly to the rope and I'll pull you up." The people were
so overjoyed with being rescued that they scrambled to get up. As
they were pulled higher and higher the air got brighter and sweeter.
Those who reached the top were awestruck at the dazzling beauty
of warm sunlight.

When the leaders saw their people getting away they did everything they could to stop them. They began torturing and murdering some in order to scare them away from the rope. But once the people had seen the light nothing could stop them in their zeal to reach the top. More and more of the multitudes made their way up the rope

and out of the pit!

Many years later when the leaders were succeeded by new younger rulers the problem still persisted. Their people were still paying no attention to them and escaping. So they came up with a new plan. After consulting the enemy they decided the best way to stop the outflow was to make the pit more attractive! So they set up all types of entertainment; TVs, videos, arcades, games, comedians, comfortable sofas and all sorts of distractions to make them forget about the rope. By incorporating these things into their religion, it worked wonderfully! Through their indulgent teachings, hardly anyone took hold of the rope anymore. They pointed out how hard it was to hang on, how dangerous it was, and because it was so high no one really knew what was up there anyway. They said the best way to have good religion was to not make any trouble, [and those heading to the rope always made trouble!].

In order to make things still more attractive to the cave dwellers, insidious men began to teach that whatever self-indulgent dreams they could imagine they could have if only they believed hard enough. This teaching became very widespread and caused many to abandon the rope. Why be bothered with the difficulty of climbing and hanging on if they could be just as happy staying where they were? After all weren't they promised by leading men that they could have everything they desired right there? The new doctrine became even more twisted as some began to say that the light of their teaching was the real light. They began to claim "This is the light, we are on the surface. It's all here, everything you ever wanted." Many were taken in. Others were downcast and confused. They were expecting the day to be much brighter than what they were seeing! And yet with so many people proclaiming the glories of the cave they were unable to remember all that their rescuer had said about the wonders of the true surface. Eventually they were able to convince the people that there really was no rope at all. It was just something dreamed up by fanatics. They carefully arrayed their various worship houses around the hole so that no one could get close enough to see the light. Everyone looking for the light had to go through them.

Meanwhile the Maker had determined a time to be set for the end of his enemy and all those who were deceived by him. A huge boulder had been rolled to the edge of the hole. When it was set in place no one would ever escape again.

Millennia later, he gave his last call. The time was at hand. Those who didn't get distracted could still be rescued, but shortly the rope would be lifted and the stone rolled in place forever.

A PICTURE OF OUR SALVATION

The apostle Paul tells us in his letter to the Philippians [2:12] that we are to work out our salvation with fear and trembling and to hold fast to the word of life [2:16]. Though we are truly saved by God's grace, yet we are instructed to be sober, tenaciously holding on to Jesus.

"Work out your salvation with fear and trembling"
"For it is God who is at work in you both to will and
to work for His good pleasure."
"Holding fast to the Word of Life, so that in the day of Christ
I may have cause to glory."

The illustration in the story describes falling into a pit. While we sit there helplessly someone comes along and finds us. In our excitement we exclaim "We are saved!" And that is certainly true. However we are still in the pit. That is, we are still full of sinful desires and surrounded by deadly dangers. We are saved in that we trust the one who found us will help us out. We are saved in the hope of actually being rescued. The apostle Peter says it like this:

"Therefore gird your minds for action, keep sober in spirit,
fix your hope completely on the grace to be brought

177

to you at the revelation of Jesus Christ." 1Peter 1:13.

The apostle Paul puts it like this:

"For in hope we have been saved." Romans 8:24.

He goes on to say that we hope for what we don't see yet, meaning there's a part of our salvation we are still waiting for. What both men are referring to is that though we are saved, we are not fully out of the pit until we set foot on that celestial shore. In the mean time we are to conduct ourselves with careful attention to God's Word. John Bunyan's 'Pilgrm's Progress' gives us a good picture of this. Peter says further;

"And if you address as Father the one who impartially
judges according to each man's work, conduct yourselves
with fear during the time of your stay on earth." 1 Peter 1:17.

This is a most excellent picture of our salvation.

GRACE AND FAITH

Make no mistake, we are truly saved when we meet Jesus. When we earnestly repent, the Father forgives us of our sin and clothes us in Jesus' righteousness. If we die then, in a state of repentance and faith in Jesus we can be assured of the Kingdom of heaven. However while we are still alive we are, as the great hymn writer said, faced with 'many dangers, toils and snares.' There are all types of insidious temptations trying to turn us back from following our Savior. That is the Pit of Sin which we are born in. There is outward sin, hidden sin, pride, worldliness, lusts of the flesh and passions of all sorts that wage war against our soul. While we are still alive on the earth ours is a constant battle to hang on to the salvation of our God. Hebrews 2:3 says *'how shall we escape if we neglect so great a salvation.'* This refers to Christians being caught up in the passing distractions of the world and by doing so neglecting the things of God. Again, we are instructed we must *'hold fast our confidence and the boast of our hope firm until the end. [Heb. 3:6].* And, if we are *'putting to death the deeds of the flesh we shall live' [Rom. 8:13].* We must fiercely and determinedly hold fast to Jesus till we are safely home with Him. That is the glorious land at the surface. While we are ascending from the pit of sin it can be a long and difficult climb, but we must hold onto the rope. Ours is to press on in faith holding onto the grace of

Jesus' salvation. Consider the very sobering words of Hebrews when it says; *'You have not yet resisted to the point of shedding blood in your striving against sin' Heb. 12:4.*

THE ROPE

This leaves us with a number of difficulties, because it is a long and treacherous climb. To begin with, as we take hold of the rope, we will find that other people in the pit will grab on to our feet and try to pull us back down with them. It is hard when it is friends, but it is terrible when it is your own family - mother, brothers or sisters. After all, it is a radical departure from what they have seen in the past. For you to abandon your previous lifestyle to follow Christ will definitely draw their attention. They will try to convince you that you're taking things too seriously and that God would never expect such things from you. They will accuse you of being high-minded and thinking you're better than everyone else. Misery loves company, so when you start to leave, you will face resistance. You might even be confronted with open hostility as you proceed.

In addition to this, there are creeping vines which grow prolifically at the bottom of the hole. Those vines wrap themselves around you and cling to you like tentacles. These are the parasitic vines of the cares of the world. Your involvement in the world and attachment to the things of the world become snares that won't let you escape from your dungeon. Your feet are entwined with cords of the desire for worldly accomplishment and suc-  cess. One by one they must be snapped so that your ascent can be unhindered. If even one remains, it prevents your upward movement. While Jesus is pulling up on you, your attachment to earthly success threatens to pry you right off the rope!

The next thing you must do is let go of anything you are carrying in order to firmly take hold of the rope. You will find it impossible to climb with a TV under your arm! We think we can be saved and still carry all sorts of things up with us. But it is not possible. You must let go of everything to ensure a successful climb. If you try to store things in a backpack, the weight of it will eventually wear you out. Better to proceed unhindered!

AN INTERESTING EXPERIENCE

As a young man, I once had the unenviable experience of literally being in this predicament. With a few Christian brothers a spelunking adventure was planned [that is, exploring little known caves]. We descended into a dark crack of the earth. This was a not well-lit tourist cave we were exploring! As we went lower and lower into the earth, we came to one point where the bottom literally fell out from under us. There was a large cavern right below us and the floor was about 40 feet under us. If you were standing on the bottom, we would have been coming through the ceiling of a cathedral sized room! Getting down was not too difficult, but when it came to returning to the surface it was a different matter. We climbed up the side part way with the aid of a rope but at one point we had to swing out over the chasm and climb the rope hand over hand to safety. It was a hair raising experience which, as you can see, I never forgot. When I think about this story and the importance of holding on tightly, that's what I think of. What would have been seemingly impossible for me to do under normal circumstances, I was able to do because my life depended on it! In our walk with Jesus much more than our earthly life is at stake and so we make the necessary sacrifices.

A STRANGE SIGHT

We in the modern church make much of the *experience* of being saved. As we look up from the pit and see Jesus' face we are overjoyed. We shout hallelujah, we're saved! Immediately everyone breaks into great delight and singing. Not that these aren't good things, but the focus can many times shift from the job at hand which is, through faith in Jesus, getting out of the pit of all our sinful desires and worldly distractions. We invent all types of music, singing and dancing to express our joy at being found. Often there is great commotion and loud exclamations of thankfulness. Meanwhile, Jesus has quietly lowered a rope and is waiting for someone to take hold of it. But, in all the excitement, nobody even sees the rope! If anyone even suggests that "This is serious, let's grab on and get out of here," they are accused of being faithless and having no joy. It must be a strange sight from heaven to see multitudes of people rejoicing in Jesus and nobody hanging on to the salvation He lowers down to them! If the apostles Peter and Paul clung desperately to the rope and considered it no small matter to arrive safely at heaven's door, how much more ought we conduct ourselves with a reverent fear during our time on earth?

BACK ON THE ROPE

Many more snares await us as we continue our upward journey. Once we manage to get past the people who would try to dissuade us from going up, and by taking the Sword of the Spirit we have severed the pit vines that were wrapped around our legs, now there are further trials that threaten to impede our progress. For one, the moment we relax our grip we begin to slide back down into the pit. There is no static place where we simply exist. If we aren't holding tightly to Christ, we are slipping down. If our  hands are slippery because the grease of pride is on them, we'll find ourselves back down on the bottom in no time. Another common snare comes in the form of meeting someone part way up. We might see a desperate looking individual that just happens to be an attractive member of the opposite sex. They are calling to you and you feel you are strong enough to take them up with you. So you let go of the rope for a moment to 'help' them and down you plunge. What you didn't know was that the enemy has not stopped his efforts to keep you from reaching the surface. He has devised every sort of trap to make sure you don't get out. A non-Christian boyfriend or girlfriend is one of his favorite ploys. You meet someone you're attracted to

181

along the way and immediately think you're strong enough in God to go out with them or marry them. That he or she is not a committed Christian doesn't stop you. Many, many potentially fine Christian women have been sabotaged by this reasoning. The most fortunate ones might even have a happy enough home by normal standards, but their fervent relationship with Jesus is cooled and a thousand compromises begin to threaten even their own salvation. The Enemy doesn't want to lose anyone; the non-Christian mate is one of his most effective tools.

On our way up we also pass many enticing things that will make us want to let go of the rope for a moment. A staircase has even been built into the wall halfway up! As we pass by, it seems to be a much easier way and it appears to go straight up. What you don't see is that the stairs ascend until just out of sight, then plunge abruptly into the abyss. There is no easy way. If you are tempted to think that God doesn't require this type of commitment from you, that is the easy staircase. Jesus warns us that the gate to heaven is very narrow and the way to hell is broad and wide for the many who choose the *easy* way.

Also as we near the top we might pass a group of people who have gathered in a large opening to congratulate us. They are celebrating your success and honoring your great accomplishments in getting so high. Many a man who has begun the climb, foiling the Enemy's plan to keep him down, has faced an even more difficult challenge as he neared the end of his course. The Enemy changes tactics as you approach the finish line. Now rather than hindering you, he now heaps accolades upon you. The glory is yours! The people have recognized your great spiritual gifts. You are recognized everywhere and highly esteemed. Beware! Proverbs 27:21 says a man's heart is tested by his reaction to praise. Those the Enemy can't stop by force or deception he can often bring down by praise. The worst part is he can also bring down with you all those who were looking to your example. So we must look to our defense. Our defense is this, that we keep our eyes straight up, focused on our Rescuer. We firmly keep in mind that though we have hung on, it was the Savior who has mercifully sacrificed Himself and is pulling us up. We remember that it was our sin that got us in trouble to begin with and without the miraculous cleansing of Jesus we could have never, ever been able to hang on. Humility is our defense.

For those alone who have thrown aside all else in order to grasp the rope firmly is the sweetest peace of knowing that the way goes upward! With every passing moment Jesus is pulling them up. They are leaving death behind with each passing day. For them the darkness is almost over, the day is at hand. Soon they will be standing next to their loving Savior, side by side. The pit will be just a memory and the glory of the sun and fresh air and all of heaven will be theirs.

"And this do knowing the time, that it is already the hour
for you to awaken from sleep; for now salvation is
nearer to us than when we believed.
The night is almost gone, the day is at hand."
Romans 13: 11 - 12.

LESSON 25

KEEP SEEKING THE THINGS ABOVE

TWO EXTREMES

Before we go further let me clear up a few doctrinal issues to make sure no one gets sidetracked. What we have discussed in the last lesson is that in some ways our salvation is a partnership. This is an area in which we must have great care unless we should ever think that any part of our redemption is based on our own merit. At the same time we are most emphatically urged by scripture to 'work out our salvation.' Jesus Himself places great emphasis on *doing* the things of God. Over the years two extremes have emerged which have kept the church from being more effective.

The first is too much attention to our part. This promotes a grace-less religion that is based on all type of religious activity. This extreme has kept the church in bondage for centuries, through the dark and middle ages. People who are earnest about God, work hard on being good or doing religious things but never have the joy of the full assurance of salvation. Because that went on for so long, we have now gone to the opposite extreme. It is commonly understood now that since Jesus did everything for our salvation, there is practically no requirement from believers at all. That is true, but only in one sense. Jesus went to the cross to redeem us [in that sense He did it all] but He also specifically states that those who would come after Him must also pick up their cross and follow Him. But instead, once we have received Christ, the church as a whole is now lazy in their approach to living for Christ. Since Jesus did it all, there is nothing to strive for! We rest and say Jesus paid the price; because we raised our hand during an altar call or grew up in a certain church there is nothing left for us to do. The end result is that God's people are in some cases indistinguishable from the world. We have gone too far.

THE FARMER

God's grace is that He pulls us up out of a hopeless pit. Our faith is that we hold on tight. In this way it is helpful to think of it

184

as a partnership, even though in a strict theological sense we would never consider our works as adding anything to the completed work of Christ. But similarly, though it is God who saves the lost by His grace, yet He uses human vessels to convey the truth. It is in that sense, a partnership. In just the same way God brings forth fruit from the fields. It is impossible for any human to make something grow. As the Word puts it, 'God provides the increase.' Yet at the same time in His glorious wisdom God makes man a partner! Man must go out and till the soil, plant it and care for it. Man plants and God causes growth. Partnership. God is the *cause* of our desire to love and to serve Him, but He does not pick us up from our bed and deposit us on our knees to seek Him. He works on our heart and we do the immediate practical things that need to be done. We work together with Him, though we are careful never to give merit to ourselves. In this way we will have the right mindset. We will not be accused by God for being a slothful [lazy] servant, and at the same time we recognize the deep truth of Philippians 2:13;

"For it is God who is at work in you both
to will and to work for His own pleasure."

To God be all the praise, honor and glory for calling us to Himself, for giving us a desire to seek Him and for giving us the promise of eternal life!

ONE LAST ISSUE

One more issue that I want to address is that we are not promoting the idea that we will obtain perfection in this life but we are to *strive* for perfection. We hold up as a holy standard Jesus' words [Matt. 5:48] that we are to be perfect as our Father in heaven is perfect. That is the measure which we must go by. But God in His wisdom has allowed us to have 'feet of clay' as it were up until the time we die. We must contend with our reluctant human nature right up till the end. This serves the very important purpose of keeping us humble and dependant on our Savior at all times. The important thing is that we are holding on to the rope. If we are holding on, meaning that we are, in faith, seeking Him to cleanse us from sin, when we die, that cleansing will be completed. By holding on we are earnestly contending for the faith. Some of the greatest saints who have ever

185

lived, died with the words on their lips, "Precious Saviour forgive me the chiefest of all sinners." They had a proper understanding of who they were before God and it kept them wonderfully humble right up to their entrance to heaven. With these issues addressed and understood we will continue.

KEEP SEEKING THE THINGS ABOVE

"If then you have been raised up with Christ,
*   keep seeking the things above where Christ is seated*
*   at the right hand of the God.*
Set your mind on the things above not on the things that are
*   on earth.*
For you have died and your life is hidden with Christ in God.
When Christ who is our life is revealed then you also will be
*   revealed with Him in glory." Colossians 3:1-4.*

In a previous lesson we discussed the things which separate us from a vibrant relationship with Christ. Among them were the passions of the flesh. At the same time we explored the lawful pleasures which God has given to mankind and determined that it was a mistake to think that God did not want His people to enjoy any pleasures of the earth. We then tried to distinguish between lawful pleasures and unlawful passions. Lawful pleasures become sinful passions when we exceed the limit set by God. But that limit is hard to define and no written law can adequately or accurately define when an individual may cross it. Now as we study the pertinent words of Paul in his letter to the Colossians we will show a better way to keep from sin in our enjoyment of God's good earthly things. And this is it: the simplest way to prevent lawful pleasures from becoming idolatrous passions is by seeking the things above. Here are the rules:

We enjoy the pleasures of the earth but we don't seek them.
We seek the joys of the Spirit instead.

We pursue spiritual joy rather than earthly pleasure.
When God grants earthly comfort, enjoy it in a spiritual way.

186

What does this mean? Our heart is where our desires are. If we are actively seeking the pleasures of this world, they take the place of God in our lives. God wants us to desire Him, not the things He created. Seeking the things which God made instead of God Himself is idolatry. It's having false gods before Him. While we are pursuing the true things above, God grants us many comforts - good food, soft beds, warm clothing etc. When He does, it is our duty to enjoy them in such a way as to be drawn to Him. In other words, we enjoy them with gratitude. We thank God  for the good He has given and our hearts become tender towards Him even in our comforts. If a father gave a special gift to his child, the child could either be totally caught up in the present or he could be thrilled with the gift and also overwhelmed by the idea that the father had done such a nice thing for him. One is merely earthly pleasure, the other is earthly pleasure enjoyed in a spiritual way.

SET YOUR MIND

When Paul says, "set your minds on the things above, not on things that are on earth," he means first and foremost we are instructed not to seek the pleasures of the flesh, that is, all the things our body craves. Seeking those things occupies nearly every waking moment for those who live natural lives in the world, so it is not an easy thing to change our focus. It takes a bold determination to seek the things above. We are to become dead to the obvious sins of the flesh which are immorality and passions, and we are to be seeking the pleasures of the Spirit or the 'things above' instead.

God in His wisdom has granted that the necessities of life are also a form of pleasure. Eating and drinking, among others, are pleasant things. If they weren't, most humans wouldn't do them! There is no virtue in abstaining from all physical pleasure as we have said but the key is we must not seek it. Again here is a good rule to follow:

We are instructed to avoid sin.
We can enjoy, but not seek the pleasures of the flesh.

187

If we do these two things we will do well. We are not to *seek* after the obvious delights of eating and drinking and comfort, though in Christ we can enjoy them and be thankful for them. If we have a strong desire for them, they have become our chief goal and replaced God as the pleasure of our life.

We are allowed to enjoy the things of this world,
But only when we are seeking the pleasures of the Spirit.

THE PLEASURES OF THE SPIRIT

Now we get to my favorite part of our spiritual training course, the pleasures of the Spirit. I mentioned several lessons ago that our Fellowship of the Unashamed commitment has two parts to it. The first consists of avoiding sin and voluntarily abstaining from the pastimes of the world which cause us to fall asleep to the things of God. These we have covered carefully. The second half of our commitment involves filling up those spaces with the delights and pleasures of the Spirit!

In our world we have two types of enjoyment. They are the pleasures of the flesh and the joys of the spirit. These two set themselves at odds against one another as Paul says in Galatians. They cancel one another out.

"But I say walk by the Spirit and you will not
carry out the desire of the flesh.
For the flesh sets its desire against the Spirit
and the Spirit against the flesh;
For these are in opposition to one another,
so that you may not do the things that you please."
Gal. 5:16-17.

If we pursue the pleasures of the flesh we automatically eliminate the joys of the Spirit. It's a law. So if we indulge in worldly pastimes, we will pay the price of sacrificing spiritual joys.

THE PRICE OF PLEASURE IS THAT WE SACRIFICE JOY

Pleasure involves only the animal part of us. We can see pleasure when we feed our pet. They attack their chow with an enviable enthusiasm! Similarly we can indulge in physical pleasures, but these are low things that we share with the animal kingdom. The things of the Spirit are elevated joys that cause the truly human part of us to soar. They are heart pleasures which come about by closeness to God and love for those around us. The joys of the Spirit are exquisite and nothing of this earth can compare to them! How we delight in these joys is the barometer of our relationship with Christ. However, be on guard, as I mentioned if we seek the fleshly pleasure, the joys of the Spirit will grow distant to us. Here are some things to consider:

- Where you might at one time have taken great delight from your time with God, now you find it is not exciting anymore. Check your life. Are you indulging in the pleasures of the flesh?

- Where you once looked forward to going to church, now it can be a drudge. Check your life. Are you indulging in the pleasures of the flesh?

- Where you used to look forward to Christian fellowship, now you avoid it. Check your life. Are you indulging in the pleasures of the flesh?

- The excitement of living and learning are gone. Check your life. Are you indulging in the pleasures of the flesh?

If you are experiencing any dryness in your spiritual life you will find in almost every case that you are habitually indulging in some worldly pleasure. Worldly pleasure kills spiritual joy. This is unavoidable because it is part of God's system of law. *"God is not mocked whatever a man sows, that he will also reap."* If we sow to the flesh we reap corruption, if we sow to the Spirit we reap life. Our greatest snare is that if we are walking along with Jesus and then indulge in some worldliness, the effects are not immediate. If we have been sowing to the Spirit we have something of a spiritual reserve, so to speak. We engage in some earthly

pleasure and our spirit doesn't seem to be affected by it. So we do it again. There lies the snare. Though it may not be an overtly sinful behavior, it still is sowing to the flesh. Every seed we plant comes up. Every single seed. So each and every time we *seek* something that gratifies our fleshly human nature it is a seed planted which will spring up and cause us to reap corruption. And what is the corruption? It is a deadness to the things of the Spirit. But, it is not a deadness that comes from having a spear driven through you, it is a deadness that is like chloroform. Once you breathe it, it makes you drowsy then puts you to sleep and finally kills you. Such is the danger of worldly indulgence. As a shepherd and one concerned about your soul, I must repeatedly warn about the dangers inherent to worldly pastimes, worldly movies, worldly entertainment and obsession with electronic media. Many, many Christians have lost all joy and victory in their lives by the creeping influence of fleshly indulgence that has come upon them slowly and imperceptibly. If you remember only one thing from this study, let this be it.

As we take the plunge and enter a lifestyle that has put the worldly distractions behind us what are the spiritual joys which God now makes available to us?

EMOTIONAL JOYS

The Bible says that there are infinite joys in God, many of which we can't even know about at this time. Paul says that the joys of heaven are unspeakable, that is, we can't even comprehend them now. But there are some joys we can know about now and we'll go through just a few.

First, there are definite emotional joys that come simply from being close to God. When our soul is at home with its Maker, it is at rest and content. As the Psalmist says;

"Like a weaned child rests against his mother,
My soul is like a weaned child within me." Psalm 131: 2

This is a delightful comfort that comes to us when we spend time with God. It is not limited in any way to our outward circumstances. In fact, the greater the storm around us, the greater the comfort He provides. Few have been through trials worse than David as he was relentlessly pursued by his enemy for many years. Yet he called God his 'stronghold' and his 'refuge.' He says in Psalm 16,

"In thy presence is fullness of joy.

In thy right hand there are pleasures forever."

David was not dealing with allegorical enemies as we might today when we pray that God would deliver us from the enemy. When David wrote Psalm 27 he was literally surrounded by an army of thousands of men. Each of them had only one thought, to kill him! Yet in spite of this he says he was confident and his heart did not fear. David had learned the secret of being close to God. He knew that despite an army encamped against him he could have peace and comfort by drawing close to God. In the midst of his circumstances he writes [Psalm 27:4]:

"One thing I have asked from the Lord and that I seek;

That I may dwell in the house of the Lord all the days of my life,

To behold the beauty of the Lord and to meditate in His temple."

He knew that the presence of God was a real place. It is not merely a figurative drawing close to God. God is a person and when we 'draw close to Him, He will draw close to us.' He speaks directly of this matter in the next verses:

"For in the day of trouble He will conceal me in His tabernacle;

In the secret place of His tent He will hide me.

He will lift me up on a rock." Psalm 27:5

THE SECRET PLACE OF THE MOST HIGH

This secret place of the Most High is the hidden weapon of defense that is ours as children of God. It is a quiet place of joy into which we can run no matter how awful the trials are that might befall us. The door is never closed to us. As we hide in that secret place all the panic and fears subside. All the wounds are treated and a deep, quiet joy returns to us. One of David's thoughts is particularly relevant to us. He says in Psalm 31: 20;

"Thou dost keep them secretly in a shelter from the strife of tongues."

There is little today that causes more pain than the criticism directed at us from family, boss, friends or Christian workers.

It can be devastating. The worst part is we don't seem to be able to get past it. The words keep coming to us and the wounds stay raw. Jesus' presence is the healing ointment for those hurt places. We draw close to Him in the secret place of the Most High and a tangible peace fills us and soothes us. Nothing in this world can compare to that quiet place in God. It is unfortunate that so few Christians even know that place exists. It is entered by spending a prolonged period of time with Him. If we simply fire off a prayer to Him, He might answer it, but we will not have a sense of His comfort that comes only from spending time with Him. David knew the secret place and spent much time there.

GLADNESS

But it is not only quiet joy and strength that God offers us, He also gives us gladness and joy! As we read yet further in the same Psalm we find David saying,

"And I will offer in His tent sacrifices with shouts of joy.
I will sing, yes, I will sing praises to the Lord." Psalm 27:6

So it is right and proper to give thanks to the Lord with our whole heart, because He Himself puts a well of joy within us. I have often said that if you look at the happiest person you have ever seen, he or she, without exception, will be a Christian who is walking close to Jesus. Joy is an inevitable by-product of a life that is given over to Him. How could it not be! God is the Fountain of Life. He is the River of Delights. He is the sum of all beauty and excellence. If we draw close to Him, these properties automatically become ours! It is a poor analogy, but when people in the world want to become elated, they spend time drinking alcohol. The effect of the alcohol is a given. If you drink it, it produces a stimulating effect. In somewhat the same way, if we earnestly seek God, we are drinking from the pure wells of salvation. Drinking that Living Water produces a definite effect. It causes the spiritual man to

become elated and joyous. It is a given. Whereas the intoxication of the world is numbing and produces many awful side effects, drinking from the Fountain of Life brings crystal clear understanding and exquisite pleasure. Again, don't take my word for it, try it yourself! Jesus is joy.

Try this little experiment. When you plan a get together with friends, especially friends from church, you are taking a chance that the evening may be flat. It may end up rather stiff or uncomfortable. If you will be so bold as to introduce Jesus into the party you will be amazed by what happens. Jesus is the life of the party! If He is sought and included in the get-together, you will find it a most pleasant and enjoyable event. Jesus brings life and joy wherever He is and He delights to bless fellowship times! Remember that if you are one who likes a party.

LESSON 26

JOYS OF THE INTELLECT

Another area that God delights to bless us in is the joys of the intellect. It tends to be a rather neglected area of the church today 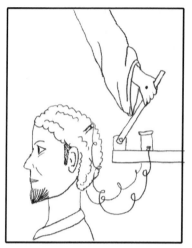 because so much emphasis is currently placed on the joys of worship. But the joys of Godly study can equal or surpass the emotional joys. God desires to take that bit of neglected hardware that fills the inside of our heads and fire it up. What He has given us is the most complex and sophisticated computer gear imaginable. It is capable of things actually beyond our imagination. The tiniest part of a human brain is infinitely superior to the greatest supercomputer. God made it. That says it all. You may feel yours is a little dull right now from lack of use, but if you give it to God He will service it for you and you'll be surprised how it jumps into life.

The key is to take the beginning step. First things first. The devil knows that the human mind is capable of wonderful things - *your mind* is capable of wonderful things. His great challenge is to take that amazing hardware and render it useless. All he has to do is capitalize on the Laws of Thermodynamics. Part of those laws state that unless energy is exerted, all things tend to break down. Higher forms degenerate into lower forms and not vice versa. This law explains why our vehicles rust away and break down unless they are constantly maintained. Our human vehicle is just the same. If it is not continuously maintained, it will also break down. Our brain is exactly the same. Unless force is exerted on it, it will break down. The higher form will degenerate into a lower form. All your enemy has to do to make your mind useless is to make sure you don't use it. It will *naturally* begin to decompose.

194

THE GARDEN

The Puritans were acutely aware of this process, so they worked hard at 'mind maintenance.' Their strict attention to educating their children was based on the fact that they knew anything that was untended would go to seed. It was clearly evident in their gardens and so it was no mystery to them. If a garden were left without proper attention, it would be full of weeds and the winter's vegetables would be lost. So, special care was given to the garden in fertilizing it, plowing it up, weeding it and watering it. If these things were properly done, they could expect wholesome produce.

They tended their children in much the same way. They considered a child's mind to be fertile soil which if properly fertilized, plowed, seeded, weeded and watered would produce great things. They were right! On the other hand if those things were neglected the produce would be ruined. That's where we are today. By negligence in weeding and watering, minds everywhere, young and old, are going to seed.

Today, instead of fertilizer to enrich the soil, we pour kerosene on it! In days gone by the young mind was trained to receive knowledge. Now it is left to its own devices, being ruined with every type of ungodly video game, TV, entertainment and worse. Where a mind would formerly have been seeded with stimulating books and knowledge, now we ac-

tually *plant* weed seeds. The books which were previously used for primary grades [take for example the McGuffy Readers] were far beyond our current college level both in content and vocabulary. Now, we expect nothing of our children, and so we get what we expect! We assume everyone has a short attention span and can't comprehend anything, and so they don't.

Where they would have diligently weeded, we now just let things grow up 'naturally.' We somehow expect an untended garden to bring forth flowers! The weeding was discipline. Their little minds were made to be attentive and focus on their lessons. The result? Their brains grew.

Watering was also vital, without which nothing can come up. The watering was the Word of God and prayer which was mixed liberally into the program. Since God in everything provides the increase, when He is removed, all real growth stops. So much for the state of modern education. The question is, what do we do now?

WHAT DO WE DO NOW?

Though many brains have been sadly neglected today, the wondrous thing is that nearly everything that was lost can be restored. God has indeed made our minds like a garden. The soil is still there and if it is properly worked, delightful things can still come forth. So the first step in reworking that patch is to take all the litter and trash

out of it. You can imagine an abandoned field which has become a home to old washing machines, burnt out cars and rusty piles of scrap metal. So is the mind cluttered with every type of garbage today. Therefore, in we go and start getting rid of it! We haul tons and tons of trash out, and with each load the land becomes cleaner. We remove the filthy and blasphemous entertainment which has made our garden into a wasteland. We haul out the disgusting piles of magazines. We clean up all the litter of trivial meaningless information. We chase off the wild coyotes that fill our property with mind-numbing noise and distraction [shut off the head phones]. And lo and behold, what do we find underneath all the mess? Good soil! Though it's been polluted for years, underneath it all is good dirt. That dirt is your dirt. That is property which God has given to you for your own pleasure and productivity. It can be restored!

Next we begin to fertilize it and plow it. How do we do that? Well, fertilizing means putting nutrients back into the soil, plowing means we begin to work the earth. We do that simply by beginning to use it. We fertilize and plow by starting to read. I don't mean the little 'sound bites' used today for the attention challenged. I mean start to actually read something that you feel is too hard for you. Something intelligent and edifying. Start with small goals. You may not want to begin with Spurgeon's Lectures To My Students [and then you might!]. Start with something like the inspiring story of a Christian missionary that easily gets your attention. Where do you find something like that? Ask us, and we'll help you. That's why we're here. Or go to a used book site and look for Jonathan Goforth, Gladys Aylward, Mary Slessor and Hudson Taylor. This will get you going in the right direction. After a short while you'll find yourself reading easily and greatly enjoying it! This is tilling that valuable soil of ours by forcing it to work.

NOW FOR PLANTING

Now we are ready to start serious planting. Now we take on the once intimidating challenge of reading the Bible through completely by ourselves. That's a big part of the program at the Fellowship of the Unashamed and we'll help you. Those who consider the Bible too hard to understand are those who simply haven't read it. Once you begin, you will find the Bible is clearly written and easy to understand. God did not want His Word to be only for the 'scholars.' He wanted everyone to be able to read it for themselves, and so it is written in a way that is easily understood. Don't take my word for it, read it yourself. You'll be surprised at how riveting the Bible is.

Next comes watering the garden. If you have ever had the experience of watching a field after it's been plowed and planted, it's a wonder to behold. It is just an open expanse of dirt with no life whatsoever. The first rain falls, then the second. Three weeks pass during which you are doing nothing but staring at a barren wasteland. Suddenly in what seems like one night, the field explodes with life. There is green everywhere! Sprouts and shoots have been manufactured from dirt! That miracle takes place when the magic of God's water comes in contact with the soil. It is written into the laws of

His creation. Water and sun on dirt and seeds produces growth. That thrill is the very thing you will experience when the garden of your mind begins to sprout!

So with us, our water is prayer. Prayer falls like water on the seeds of our reading. When we have worked our soil and begun to plant good seed, if we then water it with prayer, life will come bursting forth! It's a law. By spending time with the Lord of the Harvest,  we are ensured of wonderful results. Simple prayer is all it takes. You need say nothing more than this; "Dear Father, I wish to become a good steward with the garden You have entrusted to me. Please bless my time of study and make it fruitful. Thank you Lord." That is enough to have God send delightful showers upon your labors. The result will make you laugh with joy. You will see new life start to come forth in what used to be a barren wasteland. God promised to make the barren wilderness of Israel sprout and become like the Garden of the Lord. And so He did after thousands of years of desolation. You will have the same experience. Even if your life has been desolate for many years, as you begin to plant proper seed and water with prayer, you will find amazing fruit spring forth!

WEEDING

Next comes the difficult part. No matter how well you've worked up the ground and planted and watered, while we remain on the earth, the curse of Adam is in force. That means that along with the good seed we will also find weeds popping up prolifically. Weeds are part of life. They cannot be stopped, they can only be pulled. If they aren't taken out, they will eventually overcome the good seed and choke it out. What are the weeds in our lives? They are all the distractions and meaningless chatter and trivial thoughts that come to us unbidden. They are sinful thoughts that crowd in upon us while we are trying to concentrate on reading and studying. They are the thousands of captivating things which try to get your attention off the job at hand. The process of weeding is simply the process of discipline. The discipline is in two areas.

The first is making sure you actually set aside the time to plant and water. Your enemy hates what you're doing. He's beside himself with frustration that you've actually cleaned up the yard that once belonged to him, and now delicious Godly fruit is coming up! Just like in Jesus' parable, we have an enemy who scatters weeds among our carefully planted crops, hoping to ruin everything. He will tempt you in every way to stop tending your garden so it will naturally go back to a useless state. So discipline is mandatory for a good harvest, just like with the farmers. The farmer who decides to stay in and watch TV while he should be tending his fields will have the fruit of his labor - nothing! He must be diligent to do the job at hand in spite of it sometimes being difficult or uncomfortable. We must likewise press on and do the job before us, *"studying to show ourselves approved" 2 Tim. 2:15,* in spite of it being uncomfortable on occasion.

TENDING OUR THOUGHTS

The second area where weeding is so necessary is in our thought life. Paul tells us in 2 Cor. 10:5 that, *"we are taking every thought captive to the obedience of Christ."* That can seem like a daunting job, but it must be done. During the course of a day our thoughts can take us away to some very ungodly places. They constantly wander. And have you ever noticed that they never wander to good and uplifting things? Rather they always go away from the things of God. That's the enemy's seed being thrown into your garden. It may not have anything to do with you being sinful. The devil doesn't respect the fact that you're minding your own business!

What happens after he plants a weed seed however, is very much our responsibility. We must take hold of our thoughts and bring them into subjection to God's Word. That can take Herculian effort to begin with, because our thoughts are used to roaming around freely with no restraint! Before our minds are awakened, our random thoughts virtually run our lives and, of course, since they gravitate to the lowest possible things, they take us with them. But we have a grave responsibility to put an end to that. Paul says in Romans 12:2,

"And do not be conformed to this world,
but be transformed by the renewing of your mind,
that you may prove what the will of God is,
that which is good and acceptable and perfect."

Do not be conformed to this world but be transformed by the renewing of your mind says exactly what our job is. Renewing our mind means taking those wild random thoughts and subjecting them to God. That may take more discipline than you or I have, but that doesn't excuse us. It means we have to earnestly seek God's help to clean up our thought life.

THE CROWN PRINCE

Fortunately we have another encouraging lesson from the diligent farmer. Over centuries of toil, he has found the best way to fight weeds is to plant a lot of good seed! When he does that, he finds in many cases, things work in reverse. The good seed chokes out the weeds! So also in our lives the best defense is a good offense. By constantly filling our minds with stimulating Godly material we can effectively

cause the weeds to be stunted. Over a short time as we read more and more inspiring literature, we will find that we are actually thinking about important things. Not only that, but the things that used to interest us will seem stupid and senseless.

God has really called us to a high place in Him. He has chosen us and called us to rule with Him. The crown prince of a kingdom may be a little child just like all the other children, but he certainly isn't treated the same. Where others might spend their time in silly pastimes, the future ruler must be hard at his lessons. It can seem unfair to him while he's still very small, but when he reaches an age of understanding, he realizes that he has a special job which he must take seriously. In the same way, those who are heirs of Christ do not have the same leisure to idle away their hours with meaningless pastimes. They have a job.

They have a high calling and a serious responsibility. So our position is different from those who might be around us. What is acceptable for them is not acceptable for us. God requires more of us because of the ultimate position He wants us to occupy. It has become our duty to tend our garden with all diligence, not only for our own sakes but also for those God would have us to help.

THE DOORWAY OF DIFFICULTY

As with any form of art, music or sports, there is a period of time when your new pursuit seems like it is all discipline and no fun. If you are training on an instrument, your fingers become raw and painful. If you are training for a particular sport, your muscles feel like they can't go another step as you run laps. If you want to excel at dance or gymnastics your body rebels against the hard treatment. So it is with the greatest of all our gifts - the mind. Our mind operates just like a muscle. It rebels against anything that makes it uncomfortable. When we start to exercise it, there is a time when it puts up a mighty fight. It complains and acts as though it  can't go any farther. Push it. Everything of value in this world must be entered through the Doorway of Difficulty. It is, again, one of God's laws.

Anything of value must be earnestly striven for and there will be a period of time where you will be seriously tempted to give up. This again is your old adversary hoping he can lure you back to complacency. Remember, his job is to make sure that you don't apply energy to any worthwhile areas of your life. *The couch potato is his ultimate triumph over God's glorious creation!* In the case of a couch potato he has managed to take those who were destined to a very high calling and reduced them to complete uselessness. And he didn't have to use his skillful craft at all to accomplish it. All he had to do was feed the natural laziness of man. If it's hard, human nature tries to avoid it. He simply encourages that natural avoidance of anything difficult. We see this so clearly in children. They love to play and if you suggest anything that looks remotely like work, they whine and protest. It's human nature. As those same children grow up [that's you and me] they are still faced with the nature that hates difficulty. Those who are never trained out of that stage become the couch potatoes of the world. They watch it go by but they are not a part of it. Proverbs 1: 32 says, *"The complacency of fools shall destroy them."* By our focus on the immediate pleasure of being comfortable we sacrifice everything of value. Our brains corrode, our talents are left undiscovered, our usefulness to others vaporizes. The devil loves to encourage that sort of thing. If he can get us to do nothing he automatically triumphs over us.

KNOWLEDGE IS PLEASANT TO THE SOUL

"For wisdom will enter your heart and
knowledge will be pleasant to your soul."
Proverbs 2:10

On the other hand, we have the wonderful laws of God. Those laws establish that diligent labor produces an abundant harvest. Proverbs 14:23 says; *"In all labor there is profit."* God demands that we labor first and enjoy second. For those who persist through the 'Doorway of Difficulty' amazing things happen! If you are developing one of the talents God has given you it will start to get easier. Then it will suddenly 'click,' and in a short while you will find tremendous enjoyment in exercising your gift. In addition to your own pleasure you will find that others are also given enjoyment! If your goal is to develope your ministry gifts, persist! If you can get past the point where you feel you're a hopeless case, that your efforts are useless, you will suddenly find things start to fall into place. You will become useful and it will become enjoyable! God blesses diligence. The 'Doorway of Difficulty' is a test. Blast through it.

It is the same with the use of our minds. If we can make it past the initial discouragement, we will come into a new world of delights. Proverbs 12:1 says, *"Whoever loves discipline loves knowledge."* The initial discipline is the hurdle. Once we make it over that obstacle, learning becomes a great joy. Suddenly we can't spend enough time reading and studying. There were many men and women of God in the past who report in their journals that they would be up as early as 2:00 in the morning to study. For us today that seems impossible. We wonder how they could have labored so hard. But, you'll find from their diaries that study was not their chore; it was their delight! They simply couldn't get enough of the tremendous intellectual joy which God has granted for the diligent. They had long since passed the 'Doorway of Difficulty.' Learning was not a challenge for them. They enjoyed their times of study as modern man enjoys his Sunday sports event. The difference was their hearts and minds were enlarged and their usefulness increased.

Though it might seem impossible to you right now that same heritage is yours. The keen pleasures of the intellect were never meant for the select few. God gave good brains to all men and women. The difference is only in what we do with it. If we are faithful and diligent we also will enter into pleasures of the mind which we never knew existed. And the sweetness of God is that it doesn't matter where you begin. He gives delight to children in story books and He gives delight to scholars in thick volumes. Wherever you fall between those two, God will give you incredible delights if you start to use your hardware.

WAIT FOR THE SEED TO COME UP

The point of all this is that the Fellowship of the Unashamed has two distinct parts of its initial year-long commitment. The first is to get rid of all the garbage in your life. All the outward sins must be abandoned and then all the trash in our garden must be cleaned up. So our worldly pastimes and entertainment must be hauled off, or at the very least unplugged. That's radical, I know, but isn't your soul worth it?

Then comes a period of difficulty. The things which you relied upon for your pleasure and comfort have been put away. For a season things look very desolate indeed! You have none of your old things to look forward to. You go out to work and when you return you can't indulge in the 'you' time that is your rightful reward for all your hard work. You have laid aside all the things that you look forward to! This is your Doorway of Difficulty.

Natural seed does not come up overnight and neither will your spiritual seeds. After you have cleaned your garden and begin to plant the good seeds of Godly study, you will be tested by this season. You will be tempted to give up. Your arch-enemy will constantly tell you how worthless it is to go on. It will seem empty to you and very discouraging. Just keep right in the forefront of your mind that the diligent farmer must wait for his crops to grow. Keep on doing the things you know are right. Keep planting more seed, keep watering the seed with prayer. Seek out fellowship to encourage you through this time. We're here with you. Just be patient and wait. One month goes by. You don't feel any different or any closer to God. A second month goes by and you're still faced with cravings for the easy pleasures of the flesh. But you hold on. The third month arrives and you've begun to notice that it's not so hard to read and pray now. And it's not nearly so hard to refrain from earthly pleasures. The end of the third month approaches and you begin to feel a little stirring in your heart. For the first time since you were a little child you are happy when you get up in the morning! The things of God are starting to come alive to you and it catches you by surprise.

Then one morning without any warning, you look out and the fields are green. Your soul is bursting with life! You have never felt

this way before. It makes you laugh and sing and talk to everyone about it! Now, you can't wait to get home from work so you can read the Bible and study! Your prayer times have become a fountain of life to you. Where you couldn't pray for five minutes before, now you spend an hour with God and wish you had more time! You find yourself loving the Lord with all your heart. Your harvest has come in. God has rewarded your diligence and blessed your efforts. Now you have entered a realm that you didn't even know existed before!

You have found the words of Proverbs 4:18 to be true:

"But the path of the righteous is like the light of dawn,
That shines brighter and brighter until the full day."

THE HIDDEN SPRINGS OF GOD

The amazing thing is that it's something that no one else can see, hear, taste, or feel. You can describe it, but they can't see it. It is a harvest that causes your spiritual man boundless joy and yet outwardly no one knows why you're so happy! Many martyrs have gone joyfully to their death. They have lived in the utmost of harsh conditions and yet have a joy which makes their persecutors envy them! These are those who drink from the hidden springs of God. These joys have become yours. They are the result of laying aside the worldly pleasures and then indulging in the pleasures of the Spirit. It is the narrow gate that leads to radiant life!

I have marveled many times at those who think that a dedicated Christian has no fun. They can't understand how you can live without drinking parties, video games, movies and the like. They scratch their heads in wonder. What they don't know and can't see is the matchless delight that you enjoy in the company of God. God is the source of immeasurable gladness, because He Himself is the essence of life!

LESSON 27

THE JOYS OF THE SPIRIT

"Great are the works of the Lord.
They are studied by all who delight in them.
Splendid and majestic is His work.
And His righteousness endures forever.
He has made His wonders to be remembered"
Psalm 111:2-4

Many are the delights which God showers on those who earnestly seek Him. Closely tied to the joys of the intellect is yet another blessing and that is the joy of discovery. According to orthodox Christianity, the Bible and common sense, God can be known not only through the light of His written revelation, but also through the wonders of His handiwork. Since He is the Author of all creation, He can be seen everywhere in His works. Think about what that means! The created universe with all its intricacies and marvels is actually an amazing portrait of the Creator. Each detail is a reflection of part of His personality. As we grow closer and closer to Him we will find a new awareness of His presence in all that is around us.

The scientific age with its dead materialism could not be farther from the truth. The prevailing philosophy seeks to represent the universe as mere random bits of matter floating about. By a strange set of coincidences, some matter collides with other matter, and plants and animals come into being. Not only is that highly improbable according to the laws of probability, but it also leaves out the excitement of discovering the design behind the material world. The consequences of this poor system can be seen everywhere. The sciences become empty pursuits which leave people starved for real knowledge. There is no meaning to our existence if we are simply random bits of matter! So text books become dull and minds become duller and everything goes just the way the enemy of our souls wishes. If we are not stimulated by learning, we won't study. Then our minds become couch potato minds. The enemy wins.

True reality is the complete opposite. The truth is, everything we see, everything we touch, all the great variety of smells and tastes originate from a Creator with a limitless imagination! Again, think what that actually means.

A recent issue of National Geographic showed the latest Hubble pictures of space. What is out there defies our finite brains. Glory is the only word to describe it. Billowing clouds of brilliant gases are punctuated with bright bursts of light. The dimensions? Maybe a mere 100 light years across. That's 186,000 miles per second, times the number of seconds in a year, times one hundred. That comes to 586,569,600,000,000 miles across! If you're going to visit pack a lunch.

At the same time if you happen to be fortunate enough to have a nanoscope handy and take a look through it, you will find worlds within worlds. Each tiny atom is its own solar system. And within each living cell there is a complete reproduction of the entire creature! God has made all these marvels. He is infinitely vast and indescribably small. As we ponder these things in the light of the One behind it all, we are drawn into a worshipful state. As we gaze in wonder at the works of His hands, it brings an awesome reverence.

Believers who were scientists have throughout the years delighted in the discoveries they've made. Each one draws them closer to the Maker as they begin to understand a tiny fraction the of wisdom behind the design. Proverbs 8:22-30 says of that wisdom:

"The Lord possessed me at the beginning of His way, before His works of old.

From everlasting I was established, from the beginning, from the earliest times of the earth.

When there were no depths I was brought forth, when there were no springs abounding with water.

Before the mountains were settled, before the hills I was brought forth;

While He had not yet made the earth and the fields, nor the dust
of the world.
When He established the heavens I was there, when He inscribed
a circle on the face of the deep,
When He made firm the skies above, when the springs of the deep
became fixed,
When He set for the sea it's boundary, so that the water should not
transgress His command,
When He marked out the foundations of the earth; then I was
beside Him as a master workman;
And I was daily His delight, rejoicing always before Him,
rejoicing in the world His earth."

It is my firm belief that a good part of the joy of eternity will be the ongoing study of God's great universe. Each branch of science is enough to fill eons and eons with the excitement of discovery. Our hearts will be drawn to Him as we examine the wisdom of His works. Nor, do we have to wait for eternity to taste these wonders. Once our brain begins to be limbered up, there are no end of discoveries we can make right now. Think about just these two for a moment: God made humans to breathe oxygen and breathe out carbon dioxide. He also made trees which breathe in carbon dioxide and exhale oxygen! Ponder His ways for a moment. He also formed man 'from the dust of the earth,' that is, from the dirt. So our human body is made of the elements of the earth. Hence we take vitamins and *minerals*. But, as we know the elements we are made of are inedible. You can't eat dirt. So He then created every type of seed-bearing plant, all the great variety of fruit and vegetables. And what do these tasty little servants do? They transform inedible dirt into delicious food! Amazing isn't it?

GOD'S HUMOR

But, God is not only the author of the physical universe, He is author of more realms besides. He has invented the whole spectrum of humor and emotions as well. That means when we look at the silly antics of a kitten, or laugh out loud at a playful puppy, we are seeing right into the very heart of God! Those things are reflections of His nature, they didn't just appear by themselves. He designed all those delight-

ful creatures that fill our hearts with joy. Anyone who questions whether God has a sense of humor need only to look as far as their house pet! The good humor that we share with one another, also did not come out of the blue. The clever wit we see about us is not the product of man's ingenuity, it is a gift given to us by God. It is one of His greatest gifts in my opinion. Many a hard struggle is lightened by the introduction of laughter and humor. He delights in seeing his children enjoy one another's company and clean humor plays a big part in that camaraderie. As we draw close to Him, we will begin to see Him in all these things and will share in these pleasures. Again, those who walk closest to the Fountain of Life are by far the happiest!

GOD'S INTIMACY

For those who have experienced the joys of marriage and family, we can also see God's handiwork evidently displayed. The sweet intimate moments that we share with spouse and children come from the heart of God. The tenderness we see in caring for young children accurately displays God's closeness to us. Who can imagine a more tender picture than a mother nursing a tiny one? These things come from the heart of God. Mankind did not invent them. God designed these sweet intimate moments. He is in them. He is so much more than grand, or expansive, or glorious, or creative. He is tenderhearted. He is close to us and desires to be a comfort to us. Who can not take heart from the words of Isaiah?

"Can a woman forget her nursing child and have no compassion
    on the son of her womb?
Yea even if these forget, I will not forget you.
Behold I have inscribed you on the palms of My hands;"
    Isaiah 49:15-16

He is intimately acquainted with us and knows all our sorrow. His peace is extended to us like a river, and those who draw near will 'drink their fill of the abundance of His house.' God actually designed us to have the intimacy of family life with Him!

209

Still more joys belong to those who are His. Whether we have had the privilege of marriage or the privilege of singleness, all are able to share in the bittersweet joys of compassion. As the Savior walked, so He calls His followers to walk. His mission was a mission of mercy, His walk was a walk of service. His great work of cleaning our house is for a purpose even beyond our own good. The purpose is that we might devote our lives to the good of others.

So in the midst of our pursuits, God challenges us to lay down our own agenda for happiness and embrace a higher calling. That calling to the service of others may take many forms, but each will be uniquely suited to our gifts and temperament. Some areas to which He may call us are: feeding the poor, visiting the imprisoned, providing shelter, teaching His Word, pastoring His flock, caring for the sick, bringing hope to the hopeless, evangelism, missions, monetary giving, taking in needy children, and ministering to family members, to name just a few.

As we sit in the comfort of our living room, watching the latest blockbuster, serving others can look like a real chore! It goes against

every selfish part of us and it looks so unappealing! But as we embark on our Fellowship commitment to put aside the things of the world, new life starts to spring forth. As we get grounded in the things of God, the very next step is to apply ourselves to some area of service. Don't worry, you don't have to start by street witnessing in New York City, though you certainly can if you want to. We can help you get started! Actually just a tiny little beginning is fine for starters. Pick any of the areas mentioned above and simply get involved. One of the simplest and most fruitful opportunites is to go to a nearby fast food place. With a friend and a Bible just start reading it out loud. As people get interested invite them to join you. Tell them when you'll be back. If you start, God will be faithful to cause that seed to grow. In a short while, you will

not find it so difficult to leave your comfort zone to help someone else. Next, it will begin to capture your attention. You'll find yourself thinking more and more about helping others. Finally, the seeds of your service will sprout and you will find a harvest of compassion for those in need. With that compassion is an exquisite joy which can be had in no other way. It was the joy of our Savior Himself. The Psalms describe the Messiah as *'joyful beyond His fellows' Ps. 45:7*. He had a happiness far beyond those around Him. That joy was not based on emotion, or study, or discovery. The joy which overflowed from Jesus was the joy of compassion. It is the highest joy. It is the sweetest and the saddest all at the same time. As we embrace the suffering people of this world, we take on their pain. We become one with them in their suffering. That is the sad part. The sweet part begins as we actually see God's love raise them up. Incomparable sweetness! Those who truly know their Savior obtain this joy.

I know of a couple who followed their Savior in this joyous way. After their children were raised and their family affairs settled they left their home in Texas and went to serve God in recently freed Romania. Their work consisted of rescuing children and their babies from the streets and canals of that cold country. They took them in, they made a place for them. God blessed their work. They suffered severely as they embraced the castoffs of the bankrupt Soviet system. In the midst of all that need, they had the joy of compassion. It filled them and kept them laboring at high personal cost. They didn't mind. They experienced a spiritual pleasure that was beyond this world. They shared the joy of their Savior.

THE JOY OF SELF-MASTERY

There are still more joys poured out on God's earnest seekers! Though it is impossible for the world to see or understand, a great joy is connected with doing the right thing! As you know, there is a wave of discomfort that sweeps over us whenever we sin. We can

211

rationalize sin all we want and we can say that guilt doesn't exist, but we cannot get away from God's laws! In the same way that depression and misery inevitably follows disobeying God, so joy and lightness inevitably accompanies obedience. It is a law which cannot be broken. If we do the right and good thing, joy will pursue us and overtake us! Proverbs 16:32 says,

"He who is slow to anger is better than the mighty
And he who rules his spirit than he who captures a city."

It is a great thing to gain control over yourself. Anyone can push

themselves to excel in sports, but only a real mighty man can subdue his bad attitude, his selfishness and his temper. The book of James tells us that nobody has the strength to control even their tongue! This is an obvious truth. So seeking the Lord is in order. As we submit ourselves to Him, He gradually will give control over those areas that so easily beset us. God is not looking for great feats of strength as has become popular today in many churches. He is looking for impossible feats of self-control! There's a true muscle man. That has *God* attending the arena and cheering us on! As we submit our unruly tongues to Him we'll find a sublime joy flowing into us. Nothing can compare to the thrill of self-mastery. That's what the cross is all about. The cross means ruling our spirit. It means bringing every part of us into subjection to God.

In Hebrews 12:2 it says,

"Fixing our eyes on Jesus the author and perfecter of faith,
Who for the joy set before Him endured the cross despising
the shame,
And has sat down at the right hand of the Father."

Jesus knew the joy of self-mastery. With every obedient step He took, His fellowship with His Father became sweeter. When He mentions in the Gospel of John that He would make His home with those who obeyed Him, that's what He was talking about. Obedience, that is subjecting our own impulses to do God's will, always brings with it a wonderful closeness with God. As we consistently walk with Him, He and the Father come to us and make their home with us [John 14:23]! What can compare with that joy?

CONCLUSION

We have now reached the end, or should I say beginning, and it is our sincere desire that you are now challenged to take the road less travelled.

The road set before you is the narrow road.

Few find it, even fewer want to take it. But it is a glorious road and as we've shown it is a road of great joy. Those who find it and walk a little way down the path find such delights in God that they never look back. They will never regret a single moment that they've spent following the blessed way. It is the very road the Savior walked and His footprints are still fresh on the path. For He walks it again with each new believer who decides to cast away the world, the pleasures of the world, and the approval of the world in order to gain the true riches of heaven.

It is a road filled with peril.

Those who follow after the Master will have a share in His persecution. But it is a road of rare delights. Those who have tasted those delights have displayed an unsinkable joy and unstoppable enthusiasm. You are now surrounded by a cloud of witnesses who are earnestly cheering you on and waiting to embrace you. Welcome to

The Fellowship of the Unashamed

Fellowship of the Unashamed

member

By the grace of God, I willingly accept a commitment to abstain from the pleasures and pursuits of this world in order to seek the Lord whole heartedly for the period of one year. I purpose to join with other believers to "seek the things above where Christ is seated at the right hand of the Father" by "setting [my] mind on the things above, not on the things that are on the earth."

FORSAKING THE THINGS OF THE FLESH

"Do not be deceived, God is not mocked; for whatever a man sows that he will also reap. For the one who sows to his own flesh shall from the flesh reap corruption, but the one who sows to the Spirit shall from the Spirit reap eternal life." I desire to stop sowing to the flesh which endangers my soul and therefore commit to forsaking TV, worldly entertainment, deadening secular input of all sorts, video games, unnecessary and ungodly computer input, drugs, alcohol, and all fleshly indulgence. I use for my guide the words of Psalm 101;

"I will walk within my house in the integrity of my heart. I will set no worthless thing before my eyes; I hate the work of those who fall away; It shall not fasten it's grip on me."

SOWING TO THE SPIRIT

It is my intent to use this time to earnestly seek God. I commit to a program of regular Bible reading and private prayer. I desire to enter into close communion with the Living God that I might begin to see the fruit of the Spirit manifested in my life. I commit to listening only to edifying music and enjoying uplifting entertainment. I use the words of Jesus in John 15 as a guide; "I am the vine, you are the branches; he who abides in Me and I in him, he bears much fruit; for apart from me you can do nothing." I desire to become a fruitful worker for the Kingdom of God and I am willing to pay the price of staying attached to the Vine Himself. It is the greatest joy and truest satisfaction to embrace the cross of Christ in order to follow in His footsteps.

GREATER LOVE HAS NO MAN

"If you abide in Me and my words abide in you, ask whatever you wish and it shall be done for you. By this is My Father glorified, that you bear much fruit and so prove to be my disciples." I take as my inspiration the commitment Jeremiah lived by which was to make it a point to speak to a least one person each day about the love of God. In this commitment I am able to truly enter the fellowship of the unashamed.

GOD'S GRACE

I realize that I am in no way entering a relationship with God based on my works, but I desire to obey His word "If by the Spirit you are putting to death the deeds of the body you will live." and "Do not be conformed to the world but be transformed by the renewing of your mind" and "abstaining from worldly lusts which wage war against your soul." I openly confess that I have no power in myself to adhere to this commitment, but look to the sustaining power of God and His grace alone to pursue this course. To God alone be the power and glory.

Member_____   Date_____

ABOUT THE FELLOWSHIP

This fellowship is a simple group of believers who have found that closeness to Jesus demands a price, and that He is worth the price, whatever it is. It is not a denomination. It is not an exclusive club. It is open to everyone who wants to walk the road that He walked. We want to encourage one another, hence the fellowship. We want to be bold in our testimony of His faithfulness, hence the unashamed. Though everyone is welcome to the meetings and resource materials, the privilege of joining the fellowship comes with making a serious commitment. It is a commitment to voluntarily abstain from the pleasures and pastimes of the world for one year. During that same time each one is immersed in personal study, prayer and fellowship. Those that take the bold step find their lives radically transformed by a new intimate relation with Jesus. It's our desire that one year of earnest seeking will be followed by another and another. By faltering baby steps we can proceed in the way of giants.

He said He was coming for a spotless bride. We are commanded to be unstained by the world. If you would like to join with us in this great quest, this greatest of all adventures, please feel free to contact us at:

In the U.S.
Unashamed Ministries
P.O. Box 343
Kensington CT. 06037

In Canada
162 Harding Creek Rd.
Clinton, Prince Edward Island
Canada C0B 1M0
[Home of our Bible School]
or at

THESKYS.ORG

Made in the USA
Middletown, DE
06 September 2015